The
Quest
for
Holiness

DAVID C. LONG

FROM SHALLOW BELIEF

The **Quest** *for* **Holiness**

DAVID C. LONG

TO MATURE BELIEVER

Seedbed

Unless otherwise noted, Scripture quotations are taken from the Holy Bible, New Living Translation, copyright 1996, 2004. Used by permission of Tyndale House Publishers, Inc., Wheaton, Illinois 60189. All rights reserved.

Scripture quotations marked NIV are taken from the Holy Bible, New International Version®, NIV®. Copyright © 1973, 1978, 1984, 2011 by Biblica, Inc.™ Used by permission of Zondervan. All rights reserved worldwide. www.zondervan.com The "NIV" and "New International Version" are trademarks registered in the United States Patent and Trademark Office by Biblica, Inc.™

Scripture quotations marked NRSV are from New Revised Standard Version Bible, copyright © 1989 National Council of the Churches of Christ in the United States of America. Used by permission. All rights reserved.

Scripture quotations marked THE MESSAGE are taken from The Message Copyright © by Eugene H. Peterson 1993, 1994, 1995, 1996, 2000, 2001, 2002. Used by permission of NavPress Publishing Group.

Printed in the United States of America

Cover design by Nikabrik Design
Page design by PerfecType, Nashville, Tennessee

Long, David C. (David Clifton), 1951–
 The quest for holiness : from shallow belief to mature believer / David C. Long. – Franklin, Tennessee : Seedbed Publishing, ©2016.

 xii, 120 ; 21 cm.

 Revision of the author's D.Min. dissertation, Asbury Theological Seminary, 2014.
 Includes bibliographical references (pages 111-120)
 ISBN 9781628242867 (paperback : alk. paper)
 ISBN 9781628242874 (Mobi)
 ISBN 9781628242881 (ePub)
 ISBN 9781628242898 (uPDF)

 1. Holiness--Christianity. 2. Spiritual formation 3. Christian life--Methodist authors. I. Title.

BT767 .L663 2016   248.4   2016937783

SEEDBED PUBLISHING
Franklin, Tennessee
Seedbed.com

Contents

Foreword

It is not often that a professor mentors a doctoral student whose research, organization of findings, and presentation of material achieves a publishable level. David Long's doctor of ministry dissertation did just that.

Doctor Long's approach to the spiritual life has at least three major strengths. First, it makes it unmistakably clear that there is far more to the spiritual life than acknowledging one's fallen state, accepting Jesus as one's personal Savior, and going to heaven when one dies. Going to heaven after death is not the goal of the spiritual life. The goal is to be restored to wholeness in the likeness of Christ. This is a dynamic, transformational reality nurtured through an ever-deepening love relationship with God manifested in a love relationship with others.

Second, Long avoids the pitfall of "works righteousness" that is so often characteristic of many believers' understanding of the spiritual life. It is all too easy for the spiritual disciplines essential for growth toward wholeness in the likeness of Christ to be reduced to a list of dos and don'ts. Long carefully walks the knife edge between spiritual disciplines as works righteousness and spiritual disciplines as one's loving response of abandonment to God's transforming love working in and through us.

Third, Long grounds the spiritual life in the exigencies of daily human life rather than allowing it to become something divorced from the everyday flow of life. Too often people separate their spiritual life from their secular life each having its own sphere of influence, its own definition of human identity, its own system of values, and pattern of behavior, and rarely do the two intermingle. Long breaks that structure.

I am confident anyone who undertakes a serious study (which these books deserve) will be challenged to a deeper spiritual journey, to becoming a transformed person and God's transforming presence in the world, and blessed in that journey.

M. Robert Mulholland Jr.
Emeritus Professor of New Testament
Asbury Theological Seminary
October 3, 2015

Preface

A popular recruiting slogan from the army challenged men and women with the words "Be All You Can Be." The idea was that the recruiter had something that would help the person succeed in life, at least for a period of time. This idea echoes a call spoken throughout the Bible into the lives of men and women of all cultures. It is the challenge that we who are followers of Jesus receive, but in a much more important context—the context of our eternal life.

One place we hear this call is in the letter of the apostle Paul written to the believers in Philippi, encouraging them to press on toward that for which Christ saved them (Philippians 3:12). In other words, we are to be all that Christ saved us to be. This call has in mind a two-part transformation. The first, a prerequisite to the second, is the change in our nature that we call justification, being declared right with God by grace through faith. Justification is a change in relationship that is made possible solely through the atoning sacrifice of Jesus. It is a change from being an enemy of God to being a child of God, from being lost to being saved. The second transformation is called sanctification, something the Bible says specifically is the will of God for all who through faith have become followers of Jesus (1 Thessalonians 4:3 NIV). The first transformation is about knowing Jesus as Savior. The second transformation is about knowing Jesus as Lord. It is with regard to the second of these that this book considers what it means to be all Christ saved his followers to be.

It is an unfortunate reality that many who know Jesus as Savior have missed the command to know Jesus as Lord. Knowing Jesus as Savior implies that we are going to accept and seek to live by God's standard. To do so means to live lives that are radically reoriented from our old human nature and from the destructive tendencies of the world in which we live. Simply and succinctly, we are to respond to a Trinitarian call coming to us from the Father, the Son, and the Holy Spirit. This puts us on a journey, a journey of our spiritual formation, a journey pursued in the grace of God. This is a high calling, the highest calling, on the life of a follower of Jesus. It is a calling to a life in which the disciple of Jesus is continually striving to be more like the Lord and it is anchored in God's creative design for humankind in which men and women are made in the image of God. The life of one in which the image of God has been restored will be characterized by a deep, abiding trust in God. There is no journey more demanding, but it is a journey that can be taken in joy and which leads to joy, because for the follower of Jesus it is taken within the assurance of the unbounded love of God.

As magnificent as God is in his transcendent glory, one of the most astounding revelations of the Bible is that it is his will to be in intimate communion with the pinnacle of his creation, human beings. That's you and me! The Bible is a story of this desire, beginning in a garden, passing through another garden, a cross, the resurrection, and ending with a new creation. It's easy to read the first three chapters of Genesis and pass over them quickly or think of it as a quaint story for children. But it is much more than a children's story. It is nothing less than a picture of the struggle men and women have had throughout the ages obeying God and remaining in relationship with him as our Creator. If we look closely, every person can see himself or herself in the garden of Eden relationship between God and his creation. Throughout life every person continuously faces the same question, "Do I really and truly trust God to be a good and sovereign God?"

We begin with an exploration of the missed opportunity of Adam and Eve to place their unquestioning trust in God. The result was sin, a broken relationship with God, and the curse of a fallen self. As we come to a deeper understanding of Adam and Eve, we begin to realize that the choice they made is one we have made many times ourselves. But there is hope for change, a promise of transformation. Christian spiritual formation is imbedded in the promise that the fallen self can be transformed. Transformation in the Christian life comes by the grace of God and involves discipline on the part of a disciple of Jesus, discipline that involves understanding the call of God in one's life and Spirit-guided reflection on how the believer should respond to that call. We are led to questions of how God designed us and why we rebelled. We ask who we became as our first ancestors left that first garden, and wonder how we get back into the garden. As we understand our fallen nature or fallen self, we are enabled to surrender more and more to the transforming work of the indwelling Holy Spirit. It is a high calling and a demanding journey.

The second book in this series, *The Quest for Holiness— From Deadly Sin to Divine Virtue*, draws from the ancient understanding of the Desert Fathers in order to take a deeper look into the tendencies of the fallen self. The seven deadly sins was the template used by the Desert Fathers to describe the pitfalls they faced on a daily basis. The seven virtues are attributes of life lived in the image of God. The premise throughout is that as we, Christ-followers, understand more about our fallen self, we will find there is more grace from God for change. The goal is transformation, and in all of this we are dependent upon the grace of God to become who he created us to be.

The third book in this series, *The Quest for Holiness— From Casual Conviction to Courageous Faith*, builds on the first two books by taking our spiritual formation out into daily life. We can understand the theology that underpins spiritual formation, and we can examine ourselves for evidence of the seven sins and seven virtues, but we must take this out into the world in which we live. We live out our Christlikeness, with all our successes and all our failures, in community and in the trials and tribulations of life.

As I have written this material I have often thought of the poem "The Fools Prayer" by Edward Rowland Sill, particularly the line that reads, "These hard, well-meaning hands we thrust among the heart-strings of a friend."[1] Writing comes with responsibility. It is my heartfelt desire in writing this material that it do good and do no harm. Let the Holy Spirit be your guide, your teacher, as has been promised to you (John 16:13). That is a promise in which you can place your trust. My prayer is that regardless of the spiritual maturity you bring into the reading of this book, in every chapter you will find some challenge or some insight that will draw you into a deeper relationship of trust in God. If that happens, to God be the glory.

The
Quest
for
Holiness

DAVID C. LONG

1

The Image of God

This is the heart of spiritual formation—the intentional, sustained re-patterning of a person's life after the pattern set by God when he created human beings in his image, but made possible only by divine transforming power.

—MEL LAWRENZ

We human beings share a natural, God-given curiosity that leads us to seek an understanding of ourselves. *Why do I act the way I do? Why do I think the way I think?* Deeper moments of reflection have led many of us to gaze into the majestic vastness of the universe and wonder about our significance. This can leave us with feelings of insignificance, asking the age-old questions, *Who am I? Why am I here? What is the meaning of this life?* Seeking to satisfy this desire for self-understanding exposes us to a barrage of information that purports to offer answers. Family, friends, teachers, and television tell us what we should look like, what we should think, what we should say, and what we should do.

If we turn to the Bible in this quest, we find that the biblical account of creation speaks carefully on this point. It sets forth the order of creation, the manner of creation, and even the roles of multiplication and dominion. But it is the profound self-revelation of God that humankind is created in his image that unveils the essence of humanity. God says:

"Let us make human beings in our image, to be like us. They will reign over the fish in the sea, the birds in the sky, the livestock, all the wild animals on the earth, and the small animals that scurry along the ground." So God created human beings in his own image. In the image of God he created them; male and female he created them. (Gen. 1:26–27)

Being created in the image of God is a foundational truth for our self-understanding, a truth that plays a crucial role in the spiritual formation of a follower of Jesus. It is the source of Augustine's observation that God made us for himself and our hearts find no peace until they rest in him.[1]

Accepting that there is a Creator and that the Creator designed people in his own image leads us to a lofty view of humanity. Most people would undoubtedly agree that the human race as a whole has strayed far from our original nature, but this truth of creative design remains. This revelation of something of a God-like pattern in creation stands as a beacon, a reminder of something beyond ourselves to which we are being called to return. Embedded in the creation story is the invitation to look closely at the image of God. The invitation entreats the disciple of Jesus to ask, *What is this image of God and what does it have to do with me?* The importance of the answer for spiritual formation is that it defines its ultimate goal, a goal to be pursued by every disciple of Jesus.

After the creation passages in Genesis, little is said in the Old Testament about *image* in relation to human-kind being created in the image of God. There is a statement in Genesis 5 that says that Seth was born in the image of his father, Adam. One more Old Testament reference is found in Genesis 9 regarding the killing of a person made in the image of God. The remaining Old Testament references to image are admonitions not to represent God through an image and not to worship images or idols. The reappearance of the concept of image as a design for humanity comes in the New Testament with reference to Jesus. "Christ is the visible image of the invisible God" (Col. 1:15). Still, this idea of corre-spondence in some way between God and the life and character of his people is a basic principle of both the Old and the New Testament.

This revelation of a pattern in the image of God has intrigued and perplexed theologians for ages. The early church sought to understand what part of man and woman were created in the image of God, the body or the soul, and to what extent. The meaning of humankind being created in the image of God was being explored at fundamental levels. Origen, a highly controversial figure among the early Greek fathers, concluded that the soul of humankind, not the body, was created in God's image. This led him to the conclusion that "God's image is the perfected state to which the soul is striving."[2] To speak of the image of God in humankind is to speak of our very essence. Image is not a one-time design that lost meaning after the sin of Adam and Eve. Rather, it remains the ultimate goal of human-kind and embraces the entire purpose of God for us.

Although the image of God terminology may not be found widely in the Old Testament, the teaching of human beings becoming like their Creator is frequently discussed. This is seen in references to the gift of a new heart (Ezekiel 18:31; 36:26). In the New Testament this spiritual transformation gains wonderful clarity in the person of Jesus (1 Corinthians 15:49; Ephesians 4:15; 1 John 4:17). The *new heart* of Ezekiel is a life transformed into the likeness of Jesus. *Image* as the perfected state of the soul sheds its Old Testament ambiguity in the New Testament person of Jesus.

While time and study have resulted in a greater understanding of the Genesis passages, the reversal of the fall, the restoration of the image of God in his creation, and the pursuit of a deepening relationship with God remain as the central message of both the Old and New Testaments and, hence, of spiritual formation. Author Mel Lawrenz wrote, "This is the heart of spiritual formation—the intentional, sustained re-patterning of a person's life after the pattern set by God when he created human beings in his image, but made possible only by divine transforming power."[3] This transformation, which we also refer to as sanctification, is the heart of the search for what it means to be truly human, and more particularly, what it means to be a follower of Jesus. When we pursue true spirituality we are not running away from reality; we are pursuing reality.

It would be easy to lay the concept of image aside along with other biblical concepts that simply seem to be beyond our understanding. However, as we explore the implications of being made in the image of God, its importance as a basic truth of life becomes more astonishing. God really does say he created us in his image, and this is not just a reference to kings and rulers, the rich and the powerful, "but also every peasant, pauper, and person possesses the gift of God's image."[4] This is indeed a powerful revelation.

John Calvin recognized the revelation's implications. Creation in the image of God influenced his understanding of the nature of the Christian life. It was crucial for Calvin that Christians should recognize that God's purpose for Adam and Eve is the same for all believers. God's pattern in the garden of Eden remains the pattern for today. As was true of Adam and Eve, we are all linked to God's patterning of humankind in his own image. While relevant in the lives of all people, disciples of Jesus especially should recognize that they now are being remade into God's image. All people are called by this pattern of design to a relationship with their Creator, and those who respond and become followers of Jesus are to be formed into the likeness of Jesus, "the visible image of the invisible God" (Col. 1:15). As Calvin observed, "We now begin to bear the image of Christ, and we are daily being transformed into it more and more."[5] This transformation that is so essential after the fall of Adam and Eve is both the challenge and the promise to all who come after them. This is a high calling and a defining purpose of life.

It should be evident at this point that this book is about Christian spiritual formation. Christian spiritual formation is Christocentric, meaning that Christ is at the center of it all. In a time in which there are many types of spiritual formation, it is important to remember that Christian spiritual formation is unique. It begins and ends with Christ. That is to say, it is through Jesus that one enters into a redeemed relationship with his or her Creator and it is toward the likeness of Jesus that a believer's life progresses. In the Christian faith, the fulfillment of the gift of the image of God (*imago Dei*) is inseparable from the gracious work of Jesus, both as the fullness of the *imago Dei* himself and as the means through which the image of God may be restored in our soul.

The biblical story of creation tells us that all of humanity is remarkably designed by our Creator God, but in the Christian understanding of spiritual formation, this likeness has limits. Bearing God's image in the inner person does not mean that a person is or can become divine. God will always be *other* than his creation, including humankind. This is known as *transcendence*, meaning that God is beyond and superior to all that he created. This transcendent otherness will remain throughout eternity. Still, there is a proper sense of our participation in the divine nature. God, in his gracious design, has given human beings an invisible soul that is immortal and everlasting, attributes of his divine nature. But our participation in the divine nature must be understood in a way that avoids any notion of human beings becoming God.[6] This distinction separates Christian spiritual formation from a non-Christian New Age view. Christian spiritual formation allows for oneness with the will of God and a oneness of purpose, but never a oneness of substance. The biblical presentation of this relationship "emphasizes that human beings are distinct from the wholly other God, their Creator. And yet the priestly writer in Genesis would have us believe that something in us is an icon of God."[7]

Our understanding that the call to be like Jesus lies within God's original and eternal design for humankind opens for us a deeper appreciation of God's plan of creation. It allows us to understand that the New Testament message of who we are and whose we are is firmly rooted in the first chapter of the Old Testament book of Genesis. It also begs that we ask just how Jesus is the image of God. It is observed that the New Testament speaks of Jesus as the image of God because in the life and ministry of Jesus the presence, power, and rule of God is made known.[8] Jesus announced the arrival of God's rule (Mark 1:15), and he displayed kingdom power in many of its aspects (Matthew 12:28). He lived out the words he taught to his disciples in the Lord's Prayer: "May your Kingdom come soon. May your will be done on earth, as it is in heaven" (Matt. 6:10). He was the image of God in his perfect obedience to the Father's will (John 5:19, 36; 8:28; 10:37–38; 12:49; 14:10–11). Ultimately, Jesus obeyed to the point of death and was exalted by God (Philippians 2:5–11). In all things he brought glory to God.

This example of Jesus helps us learn what the human vocation is to be like. From the life of Jesus it is understood that the human vocation embraces surrender to God, which defines both our relationship to God and to others (Matthew 6:33). M. Robert Mulholland wrote, "Union with God results in our being a person through whom God's presence touches the world with forgiving, cleansing, healing, liberating and transforming grace."[9] As reflected in the life of Jesus, spiritual formation, or sanctification, is the growth we are to experience as people who believe in Jesus—growth that moves us toward the image of God. Are you seeing the big picture? From the very beginning and throughout all of time, God has had in place a pattern and a process that flows from his sovereign decision to make us after his own image.

It was into this vocation—bringing glory to God—that the first Adam was created, but he and all his descendants have failed at the task. It was into this vocation that the second Adam, Jesus, was born. Through his perfect surrender and sinless life, Jesus fulfilled the human vocation. "In short, Christ imaged God by fulfilling the human vocation. Christians image God as they are progressively conformed to the image of Christ."[10] Jesus lived out the image of God in his daily life and ministry (Colossians 1:15, 19).

We participate in the divine image only as we live lives as true disciples of Jesus. This conveys the vital understanding that the image of God, and therefore being in the image of God, is a *dynamic* reality. When our life is lived in the image of God, it is not a motionless picture. Rather, it is a vigorous, active, and forceful life—a life that reflects the glory of God. As will be discussed in the next chapter, the fall of humankind resulted in a realignment of life, the distorted focus on things other than God. Since Jesus is the *imago Dei,* a focus on Jesus is a restored and properly aligned life focus. In Jesus "the mirror of our humanity loses its distortions and regains its proper focus on God, so that in Christ the image is restored and through him can be restored in us as well."[11]

Our creation in the image of God means much more than can be observed from a casual reading of the Genesis passage (Genesis 1:26–27). When we see its relation to our human vocation, it compels an order of life that surpasses the relatively mundane pursuits that we so often mistakenly perceive as life's ultimate goals. That short passage in Genesis encapsulates what it means to be truly human. It also provides a hint as to God's design for our destiny. "If the first Adam shows us what we are, the last Adam promises what we shall be, and the one is the fulfillment of the other."[12]

With this understanding, the full extent of the dynamic revealed by creation in the image of God begins to become clearer. The image of God is the ultimate promise for and reality of humankind; it is true personhood. As the revelation of creation in the image of God begins in the Genesis story, its conclusion is found in the narrative of God's work presented in the book of Revelation. Through that revelation comes the vision of God's faithful people with the name of the Father and the Son on their foreheads:

> Since a person's name is a manifestation of their nature, to have God's name upon one's forehead is to have one's nature conformed to the nature of God. . . . Being the people of God is a matter of having one's very being restored to the image of God. In Paul's terms, it is being conformed to the image of Christ.[13]

For a brief time the first ancestors experienced life in the image of God, but now those who follow await the day when they will be fully conformed to the image of the Son (Romans 8:29; cf. 1 John 3:2). That does not mean waiting passively through this life on earth. It is a life in which the follower of Jesus is called to actively participate each and every day:

But the end of our faith, the salvation of our souls, is the actual conversion of our whole nature into the image of Christ. The end is a person that esteems others as more important than self. It is a content and generous heart. It is a soul that has taken ownership of the spiritual climate in his or her church; that has learned to wait on God; to see with faith, to rejoice in suffering, and to suffer with the world.[14]

The marvelous grace of our Creator distinguishes us from the rest of creation. Only we are created in the image of God and invited into a personal relationship with God. It is God who defines that relationship and how we enter into it. This reality of creation justifies a very high view of humanity not only because the human race was originally created in the image of God, but also because we may be restored by God's grace to that image.

From the first chapter of Genesis, God told us who we are and who we are to become. By patterning human beings in his image, God began the revelation of the fullness of life he planned for the pinnacle of his creation. On this T. A. Smail wrote, "We are the human beings that we are through our bearing of the *imago Dei*, which is not a religious add-on to an already existent humanity but itself constitutive of that humanity."[15] In other words, who we are as human beings and who God intends us to be is expressed from the very beginning by God's creation in his image. Creation in the image of God means human beings have souls that can be transformed from a distorted image to the Creator's image. We have been made by God and for God, and our fulfillment in life comes with our alignment with this truth of creation.

Reflection and Application

1. The following definitions are used throughout this book and should be clearly understood:

   a. *Justification*: The change in status from enemies of God to friends, even children of God, that occurs solely by the grace of God when we first place our faith in Jesus (Romans 5:11; Ephesians 2:8–9).

   b. *Sanctification*: Growth in the likeness of Christ, the re-patterning of life in the image of God. In the words of the apostle Paul, it is becoming all that Jesus saved a person to be (Philippians 3:12).

   c. *Spiritual Formation*: As used herein, this is the same as sanctification. The following is a definition from M. Robert Mulholland Jr.:

   > Life is Spiritual Formation. Human life is, by its very nature, spiritual formation. The question is not whether to undertake spiritual formation. The question is what kind of spiritual formation are we already engaged in? Are we being increasingly conformed to the brokenness and disintegration of the world, or are we being increasingly conformed to the wholeness and integration of the image of Christ?[16]

2. Read Genesis 1:26–27 reflectively. Before the first act of creation, God could have created in any manner

consistent with his attributes, nature, and character. What does design in God's image say about God's view of humankind? What does it mean to you that God decided to make you in his image? What does it say about relationship with God?

3. Oswald Chambers, the author of the classic devotional, *My Utmost for His Highest*, wrote:

> Salvation does not mean merely deliverance from sin or the experience of personal holiness. The salvation which comes from God means being completely delivered from myself, and being placed into perfect union with Him. When I think of my salvation experience, I think of being delivered from sin and gaining personal holiness. But salvation is so much more! It means that the Spirit of God has brought me into intimate contact with the true Person of God Himself. And as I am caught up into total surrender to God, I become thrilled with something infinitely greater than myself.[17]

How does this devotional about spiritual formation align with what has been said about creation in the image of God? What does it say about the transformation in life that is to come from spiritual formation? What is your commitment to this transformation and what would you like it to be?

4. What would you identify as most important in your life? How do you think most Christians would answer this? How would a life aligned with this priority be lived?

2

The Fall

The crux of humankind's alienation from God lies in "the difficulty that the human heart and mind can have in genuinely trusting God as a wise creator and living accordingly."

—R. W. L. Moberly

Thomas Merton observed that the unique relation between God and Adam may be described as sonship because Adam shared God's own Spirit. "Adam, then, was meant from the very first to live and breathe in unison with God, for just as the soul was the life of Adam's body, so the Spirit of God swelling in Adam was to be the life of his *soul*."[1] Adam was not created as just one among the many and varied animals formed by God but rather as one that would choose to obey God's command.

It would be impossible to write a script that has a more glorious and promising beginning than the Genesis account of the creation of Adam and Eve in the image of God. As the pinnacle of creation, God placed Adam and Eve in a garden in which all of their needs were met, including intimacy with their Creator. It was a garden filled with permission and only one prohibition. Astonishingly, as evidenced by the space occupied on the written pages of the Bible, this best of all beginnings is followed closely by the account of sin and the fall from grace. This beginning was marred by rebellion, disobedience, and separation from God. It seems that as soon as Adam and Eve were placed in the garden they turned away from God.

The seemingly simple command guiding this relationship is recorded in the second chapter of Genesis: "You may freely eat the fruit of every tree in the garden—except the tree of the knowledge of good and evil. If you eat its fruit, you are sure to die" (Gen. 2:16–17). Don't eat from this tree, Adam! If you do, the result will be death! As long as you obey, the created relationship will continue. It sounds so simple, yet something went terribly wrong in this perfect relationship. By the end of the third chapter of Genesis, both Adam and Eve had disobeyed and had incurred the judgment of God. The simple answer to what went wrong is that sin produced a separation between the creatures and their God (Isaiah 59:2). The reality with which humanity has lived ever since is that sin has consequences. It was presented clearly in the Genesis account that to choose disobedience was to choose broken fellowship, yet that was exactly the tragic choice made by our first ancestors. They were tempted with something appealing and attractive, and they decided it was better for them than the command of God.

The power of sin is in its appeal. It presents itself to us as something desirable, something that in some way will bring us satisfaction, most often an immediate satisfaction. In some way, the opportunity presented by sin is measured against a command of God and sin is deemed more desirable. For this reason, sin is always an affront to God. Adam and Eve were made for fellowship with God and with each other, but suddenly they felt shame, distrusted God and each other, resented each other, and were banished from Paradise.[2]

The series of events which we read in Genesis 3:1–6 constitutes what some have described as the greatest theological problem in the Word of God. Considering their intimacy with God, their place in the garden, and the clarity of the command, how could Adam and Eve have disobeyed? Why would God have created them in such a way that this disobedience was a possibility? We are permitted to probe the mind of God in search of answers, but we must be willing to find peace in the faith that disobedience does not thwart the goodness of God's sovereign plan.

The familiar scene portrayed Adam and Eve in the garden of Eden standing in front of the tree of the knowledge of good and evil. The serpent, or Satan, was engaged in conversation with Eve, but note that in this particular context the presence of God was not mentioned. It *seems* as if he was not present. Although Christian doctrine holds that God is omnipresent (present in all places) and omniscient (all knowing), this first encounter *seems* to be only between Satan and the humans. Indeed, verses 8–11 tell the story as if God discovered the event at a later time. God was walking in the garden when he asked Adam,

"Have you eaten from the tree whose fruit I commanded you not to eat?" (v.11).

This absence of an overwhelming presence of God is an important element in this well-crafted scenario. Our burning question is, *How could Adam and Eve live in the presence of God in the garden and still turn away in disobedience?* The answer may lie in the distinction between the omnipresence of God and the manifest presence of God. A. W. Tozer wrote, "The presence and the manifestation of the presence are not the same. There can be one without the other. God is here when we are wholly unaware of it. He is manifest only when and as we are aware of His presence."[3] Likewise, we are reminded that, "we cannot attain the presence of God. We're already totally in the presence of God. What's absent is awareness."[4]

True to his general nature, God is everywhere. There is an impersonal presence of God that is in no way affected by prayer, belief, or obedience. The manifest presence of God, on the other hand, is the specific, selective presence of God with his people, normally as a result of prayer and obedience. We can see this in the story of Moses and Pharaoh. God was present everywhere Pharaoh was, even though his presence was unrecognized or rejected. He was also present with Moses and his people, but that presence took the form of a pillar of fire and a cloud. God was present among the Egyptians, but his presence was manifest among the Israelites. Adam and Eve had already taken a path of independence and disobedience that took them away from the manifest presence of God and brought them within reach of the tree with the forbidden fruit; it brought them within the sphere of temptation by the evil one. In his omnipresence God was present during the temptation. If Adam and Eve had been following in obedience, God would have been with them in his manifest presence and their response to the temptation could have been very different. The lesson in this is that the scenario in the garden of Eden was not unique to Adam and Eve. Rather, it is one that is repeated in the lives of their descendants every day.

How unfortunate that Adam and Eve chose to face Satan on their own. Intriguingly, while Satan tempted Eve, he never told her to eat the forbidden fruit. Instead he undermined God's trustworthiness and truthfulness. Look at the deception. Satan misrepresented God by suggesting the command was unreasonable. "Did God really say you must not eat the fruit from any of the trees in the garden?" (Gen. 3:1). Eve caught the blatant error in Satan's statement, but she was hooked by the underlying deception. Eve's heart was opened to Satan's direct challenge of God's command. "You won't die, Eve. In fact, if you eat you will actually be better." The enticement of Eve did not come to her in the form of brute force but through the relative passivity of an idea. "It was with the idea that God could not be trusted and that she must act on her own to secure her own well-being."[5] Eve was never told to disobey God, but she was told that she would be better off if she followed her own choices and that no consequences would come from her disobedience. Dallas Willard pointed to the disastrous reality of the consequences when he wrote:

When Eve through mistrust of God (3:6) took the fatal step, she and Adam did not cease to be "living beings." But they nevertheless died, as God said they would. They ceased to relate to and function in harmony with that spiritual reality that is at the foundation of all things and of whose glory the universe is an expression. They were dead to God.[6]

The story presented Eve drawing her own conclusion as to the correct action to take—obey God or seize what appeared to be a good and rational opportunity. Within this scenario we can see the essence of a love relationship in which love cannot be coerced; either party must be free to say no:

Inherent in God's "decision" to create beings in his own image was that they could know their wholeness in a relationship of loving union with God. These beings were given the freedom to say "No" to that relationship because a love relationship always leaves the beloved free to say "No," otherwise it is not a love relationship but coercion.[7]

The garden reveals the crux of our alienation from God, "the difficulty that the human heart and mind can have in genuinely trusting God as a wise creator and living accordingly."[8] Embedded in the story of disobedience is the key challenge to relationship with God that has been faced ever since, the decision of the creature to trust or not to trust the Creator. Satan is aware of this challenge and makes the trustworthiness of God the object of his attacks.

While Eve was the principal actor in the Genesis account, the New Testament blames the fall on Adam (Romans 5:12). Adam's sin changed the relationship between creature and Creator. Adam had no reason to distrust God, but he chose to allow distrust, distance, suspicion, and disobedience to enter into his relationship with God. Dennis Kinlaw wrote, "And behind the shift from trust and communion to suspicion and separation was an overriding concern for themselves."[9] Like Adam and Eve, we all have a tendency to make ourselves the center of importance. Martin Luther used the phrase "*cor incurvatus ad se*" to depict this human condition, which means "a heart curved in on itself." Sin occurs when a person rebels against the created order and takes the place of God in his or her life. Alignment, or misalignment, of life around oneself means we determine the priorities of life and we live in a way that tries to satisfy those often distorted priorities.

Look at the deceptive nature sin can have. The distinction between blessing and curse can be subtle, confused all the more by Satan's implication, "You deserve this!" Further, Luther observed that God gave Adam no rationale as to why he was not to eat from this particular tree. In addition, from the perspective of Adam and Eve, neither of the two could look at the fruit and conclude rationally that God's command not to eat was good and reasonable. The tree was beautiful, its fruit would satisfy the natural need for food, and it would give them wisdom. To the rational mind, these all seemed to be good. But if the rational mind is corrupt, mistaken ideas and false beliefs will poison life. The command was not one to be justified through reason. It was to be obeyed for the sole reason that it came from God.

It was precisely at this point that the serpent sought to drive the wedge between God and humans, this point of struggle between trust in rational human thought and trust in God. Satan tempted Adam and Eve to make what seemed to be a rational decision even though it was in clear opposition to God's command. This new scenario afforded to them the greatest opportunity to demonstrate trust in God, *obedience even when the rational mind does not understand the way of God* (Isaiah 55:8–9). Instead, Adam and Eve substituted their own human reasoning for the word of God and trust in their own rationalization for trust in God. "One of the major theological points of this story is that true wisdom comes only through intimacy with God and the attempts to secure wisdom outside fellowship are doomed to failure."[10] It also makes it clear that the deepening ability to trust God is a vital element of spiritual formation.

Some observe that the eating of the apple was, after all, not a very serious offense, making it easy for our human reasoning to tell us that the punishment did not fit the crime. Such a simple act, it may seem, should not have borne the consequence of the death of not only the perpetrators but all of their descendants. To the contrary, though, it is important that we understand that it is the seemingly inconsequential nature of the command and its breach that conveys the very point of the story. The arguable irrationality of the command combined with the threat of death upon disobeying has been understood to mean that even the slightest disobedience of the command "was and must be a totally catastrophic sin which would estrange from God not only the immediate offender but also all future descendants and indeed all future humanity."[11]

We come to the understanding that God set out a fundamental truth that defines our relationship with him. Any disobedience is sin and any sin has tragic consequences. We can understand this seemingly harsh outcome more clearly when looking at the contrast between the first Adam and the second Adam, Jesus. Matthew 4 tells the story of another temptation—the temptation of Jesus in the wilderness. Jesus had just been baptized, had heard the affirming words of the Father, and was beginning his public ministry. We are told that he was led into the wilderness by the Holy Spirit to be tempted by Satan. The first two of the three temptations that followed were prefaced with the challenge, "If you are the Son of God" (Matt. 4:3, 6). It was God the Father who, at the baptism of Jesus, said, "This is my dearly loved Son, who brings me great joy" (Matt. 3:17). Once again, as in the temptation of Adam and Eve, Satan was saying, "Did God really say?" More specifically, the tempter was saying, "If you are the Son of God, you deserve more than God is giving you. You have a right to more!" The temptations came in three forms: to turn stone into bread for his own need, to prove his identity as the Son of God, and to claim dominion over all the nations. Succumbing to the first temptation would seem to have had the reasonable, sensible end of satisfying his hunger; the second of proving that he was indeed the Son of God. The third would have been consistent with a dominion already promised in Scripture as Jesus is Lord of all.

Each of these temptations involved the sin of seeking fulfillment outside of the trusting relationship with the Father. Still, because of the promised results, we are so capable of rationalizing these as reasonable and acceptable ways for Jesus to have responded: being fed, being known, and being exalted. Although he was defeated by Jesus in the wilderness, we see Satan's tenacity when he came back with the same temptation at the cross. The same conditional statement, "if you are the Son of God," came once again through the mouths of Jesus' tormentors, challenging Jesus to come down from the cross (Matt. 27:40). It would be easy to rationalize that in feeding himself or escaping from the horror of the cross there was no harm and no fault in Jesus to be found. But this rationalization, so easily made from a self-referenced viewpoint, would obscure Matthew's depiction "of what it means for Jesus to be Son of God, in which his refusal to go along with the enticing suggestions is not marginal but fundamental to the whole meaning of his trusting and obedient sonship."[12] In other words, the obedience of Jesus that flowed from absolute trust of God was constitutive of the relationship between God the Father and God the Son. It is a relationship conditioned upon absolute trust, which is the basis for absolute obedience.

The decision of Adam and Eve of whether to succumb to the enticing suggestion of Satan was neither marginal nor inconsequential, but rather points to the very essence and intensity of the trust relationship for which and into which they were created. They were created by God and for God, which called for unswerving trust in God. Adam substituted his own rational understanding of what seemed good for what God said was good for him. John Wesley spoke of the consequence of Adam's action: "By these acts, the man and the woman flagrantly declared that they would no longer have God as their ruler. They would be governed by their own wills, not the will of God who created them. They would not seek happiness in God, but in the world and in the works of their own hands."[13] Jesus, on the other hand, sacrificed himself in obedient trust of the Father. A marked difference between the first Adam and the second Adam was their trust in God.

It becomes apparent that trust in God was the central issue in the temptation that led to the fall. As Oswald Chambers wrote, "Our problems arise when we refuse to place our trust in the reality of His presence,"[14] recognizing that an awareness of God's presence strengthens our ability to trust. Had Adam and Eve been attuned to God's presence, it surely would have influenced their actions. They had a choice, which gave them the full opportunity to trust in God. Trust in God allows for dependence upon God and, in their case, trust for food and wisdom. Distrust of God requires dependence upon oneself. This brings us to a deeper understanding of sin: Sin is our unwillingness to be radically dependent upon God "for life and breath and all things." It is, therefore, the idolatry of preferring to be "gods" rather than truly human (which was, of course, the primal temptation in Eden).[15]

Trust may at times in our lives be an easy response, but at some point a trust of radical dependence is likely to be demanded of (or offered to) all of us who are disciples seeking to be like Jesus.

Again, in the contrast between Adam and Jesus, the meaning and purpose of life is brought into clear focus. Both faced a command that from a purely human viewpoint lacked strong rational clarity. For Adam, the command was not to eat within the context of every need being provided for him. For Jesus, the command was for total surrender even to death. Trust in the Father, that God is without qualification a good and sovereign God, is the defining essence of the relationship between the Father and the Son. This trust sustained Jesus through his passion, crucifixion, and resurrection:

> It is often observed that Jesus did not answer Pilate when he asked his famous question, "What is truth?" (John 18:38). We may think of the entire passion, however, as Jesus' answer. The right human relation to the one true God is that of trusting in the life-giving power of the Spirit of the Father, even in the face of hostile enemies.[16]

Adam and Eve missed a great opportunity to grow in trust and to love and glorify God by trusting. The whole work of God in redemption is to undo the tragic effects of their decision. Through his unequivocal trust in the Father, Jesus knew the truth, lived the truth, and is the Truth. This invites us to examine the strength of our own commitment to the commands of God and the alertness we have to the opposition that might come from our own rational mind. As modeled by Jesus, we are challenged to trust God as the greatest good even when our rational mind suggests otherwise.

Reflection and Application

1. Familiarize yourself with Genesis 2:16–17. What was God telling Adam to "do"? What reason did God give for giving this command to Adam? What was the stated consequence of disobedience? When you are told to do something but are not given a reason for it, what influences whether or not you obey?

2. Read Genesis 3:1–11 reflectively. Draw yourself into the story as a close observer of the event. Where is the tree? Where is Eve? Where is Adam? Where is Satan? Where is God? Given the sovereignty of God, why do you believe he allowed this to happen?

3. The emphasis in this chapter has been on uncompromising trust in God and the difficulty human beings have trusting in this manner. What had God done that would allow Adam and Eve to trust him? What had God done that would cause Adam and Eve to distrust him? When they were making the decision of whether or not to obey God's command, what did they need to trust God for in order to be obedient?

4. What makes it difficult for you to trust God?

5. The rational mind is a gift from God. As a gift from God, it should be exercised and developed to its full potential. What circumstances are you aware of in life in which one course of action seems reasonable but the Word of God forbids it or points in another direction?

6. Considering one of those circumstances in which the rational course of action is in conflict with the Word of God, in what specific ways do you need to trust God in order to be obedient to his commands?

3

The Fallen Self and Its Consequences

Without God as the center of our identity, value, meaning, and purpose, we are imprisoned in a structure of being that must develop its own center of identity, value, meaning, and purpose.

—M. ROBERT MULHOLLAND JR.

The apostle Paul wrote to the church at Philippi that it was his desire to become all that Jesus saved him to be (Philippians 3:12). In doing so, he provided a good sense of the meaning of sanctification, or spiritual formation. This is the call into the life of every follower of Jesus: be all Jesus saved you to be. This was a driving passion in Paul's life. Yet, as we see from Paul's life, as a believer responds to this call for spiritual formation they find themselves on a battleground in which the enemy is the *fallen self*. While there are a multitude of manifestations of this fallen self, it essentially involves our willingness to play god in our life to the exclusion of the true God. It is the heart turned in upon itself rather than being oriented to and dependent upon God. It is a radical departure from the relational design God brought into being when humankind was created in his image. It is, simply, rebellion.

Adam and Eve left the garden of Eden with a nature that acted in a way very different from what God intended. Their orientation toward themselves changed how they lived and how they understood what it meant to be truly human. Their basic needs were the same—security, acceptance, hope, love, intimacy, and the like—but they had begun to satisfy these needs through their own means and for their own purposes rather than through trust in God's means. This is descriptive of the fallen self, a distorted human nature. God's redemptive work is the correction of this nature and that is the focus of spiritual formation. This being so, it follows that an understanding of our fallen self and its consequences is crucial for this journey we are on from broken relationship with our Father to restored relationship, from self-reliance to trust in God. Paul wrote of straining toward the heavenly prize to which we are being called by God through Christ (Philippians 3:14). Understanding the fallen self and its consequences will help us as we, too, strain for the prize in this journey of transformation.

The Genesis account of creation and the fall is a marvelous scenario from which we may draw vital lessons regarding spiritual formation. It helps us to know God and his purpose for us. It reveals that in God's order for creation he was the One who provided for his creation. God gave Adam permission to eat from any tree in the garden except for only one, the tree of the knowledge of good and evil (Genesis 2:17). We can be sure that God's provision was not in any way inadequate, but rather flowed abundantly from his riches. In her dialogue with Satan, Eve acknowledged this provision (Genesis 3:2). Satan set out to deceive Eve into thinking it was not adequate and that she deserved more.

God provided, and did so in harmony with the rest of his creation. But God's way of providing was rejected. At the heart of the disobedience of Adam and Eve was their decision to provide for themselves. They chose to provide their own food, their own wisdom, and their own way of living. In short, they chose to live in a way separate from God and his provision for them. This is the essential nature of sin, distrusting and choosing the absence of God.[1] Yet, in an amazing act of grace, despite this disobedience God continued to provide for Adam and Eve. He responded to their shame, which they felt as a result of their sin, by providing clothing from animal skins (Genesis 3:21). But this time the provision was not in harmony with creation. It cost the life of the animal from which the skin was taken, pointing to the broad and devastating consequence of sin's reorientation and reliance upon self. It was the first sacrifice of blood, foreshadowing a greater sacrifice to come.

We can see that it would be a mistake to read the creation passage as if it spoke only of the material needs of Adam. The reorientation from God to self was pervasive, affecting not only physical needs but emotional, relational, and spiritual needs as well. For a seemingly brief period of time, Adam and Eve lived in close communion with God. They were aware of his presence as he walked in the garden in the cool of the evening and had dialogue with him (Genesis 3:8–12). Created in the image of God, they enjoyed this close, intimate relationship. But they broke that relationship by their lack of trust that God's command was in their best interest. They made a conscious choice of disobedience, choosing self-reliance in place of trust in God. Suddenly, as the forewarned and inevitable consequence of their disobedience, they were banished from God's presence and the intimacy into which they had been created. As descendants of Adam and Eve, our fallen self continues to believe that our deepest happiness will come from living our way, not God's way, for God will not *really* provide for our happiness.

Beyond bringing about a broken relationship with God, fundamental changes in the very essence of humanity resulted as the heart turned inward toward self. Wesley thought of this corruption of human nature as a lack of original righteousness. But more than simply an absence of this quality it was also the introduction of "an active power that predisposes the tempers of human hearts toward sin and disobedience"[2] (Rom. 7:23). In other words, when Adam and Eve turned away from God and to themselves, their nature changed to one with a tendency to disobey, a bent toward sinning in which the first thought is of self, not God and neighbor. Rejection of God as the sustaining Source of being creates a void that has to be filled. A new source of our being must be found. Created beings, then, with distorted motivations from a heart bent on satisfying itself became their own source of being or the distorted source of their distorted being.

The fall involved the introduction of an active power that bent the heart toward sin and disobedience. What does this mean? This power is neither an alien possession nor an external influence that has taken control. Comedian Flip Wilson made the quip, "The devil made me do it!" famous as an excuse for all kinds of misconduct. The devil is actively engaged in tempting and luring people away from God, but we are responsible for this drive within us (1 Corinthians 10:13). It acts upon the motivations that are a normal force in the human spirit. However, this drive to satisfy human needs and demands is now carried out according to a different set of priorities, those required to satisfy the fallen self. Their satisfaction is pursued in a manner separate from God. That is the power, or distorted power, that predisposes the human heart toward sin and disobedience. This fallen self will always advocate that we put self first over God and others.

In ways that are beyond full understanding, human nature changed from one designed to live in unison with God and flourish in his grace to one that chose separation from God. A mind that distrusts God is ordered by the priorities of serving something other than God. That *something other* is the fallen self. Remember Martin Luther's definition of sin—the heart curved in on itself. In M. Robert Mulholland's book *The Deeper Journey*, we find an examination of the fallen self, or false self as it is called, and the distorted ways it seeks to achieve distorted priorities. Fundamental in this is the priority of self-glorification. This simply means we put our own needs first and hence, in a sense, worship self. Instead of glorifying God and serving of others, the fallen self steals the glory due God and turns it to itself. This occurs at a deep, basic level. For instance, it is natural for us to need to know our identity and to have a sense of value, meaning, and purpose in life. The fallen self seeks to satisfy this need, but does so in service of self. The result is the use of means that are often harmful to the rest of creation, means that include self-protection, manipulation of others, excesses of one kind or another, and self-indulgence. As a result, the fallen self becomes a fearful self—fearful of anything that might challenge the carefully constructed matrix of identity, value, meaning, and purpose by which the fallen self exalts itself. With the fallen self managing life according to self-referenced priorities, it fears that it might not be valued in the way it perceives it is due.[3]

From the instant this new reality of sin entered their hearts, a new set of priorities began to influence if not dictate the thoughts, feelings, actions, and desires of Adam, Eve, and their descendants:

> Without God as the center of our identity, value, meaning, and purpose, we are imprisoned in a structure of being that must develop its own center of identity, value, meaning, and purpose. We become controlled by the demons of performance who tell us that we are what we do. We become driven by the demons of possessiveness who tell us we are what we have. We become possessed by the demons of popularity who tell us that we are what others think of us. We become guided by the demons of power who tell us we are what we can control. Such a life is perpetually in conflict with others, with whom we must compete for performance, possessions, popularity, and power.[4]

Augustine understood this intrinsic consequence of the fall. "My sin was this, that I looked for pleasure, beauty, and truth not in [God] but in myself and [God's] other creatures, and the search led me instead to pain, confusion, and error."[5] This distorted way of life is the curse of the fall. Thomas Merton observed that while Adam sought to improve himself through the addition of knowledge (Genesis 3:6), in reality he lost the experience of goodness into which he had been created by God. He removed himself from the intended sphere of God's goodness. Adam's change in essence also meant the loss of "his immortality, his contemplation, his power over himself and over irrational creation and finally even his status as a son of God."[6] From this state of separation from God came disordered passion, ignorance, and suffering:

> He exchanged the spontaneity of a perfectly ordered nature elevated by the highest gifts of mystical grace, for the compulsions and anxieties and weaknesses of a will left to itself, a will which does what it does not want to do, hates what it ought to love and avoids what it ought to seek with its whole being.[7] (see Romans 7:15–19)

In other words, God's design for Adam was perfect, but that alone was not the end of relationship. Adam was not to be abandoned but rather this perfect design was to be continually sustained and elevated by the grace of God. Even though perfect in design, humanity still needed the grace of God to be all God created them to be. We will never lose our desperation for God.

Augustine understood that to say we are innately ruled by distorted priorities is to say we have a distorted love. He recognized the existence of two basic loves, one a love of God that excludes the opposing desires of self, the other a love of self to the rejection and distrust of God. Having been born into love of self, the follower of Jesus is called to transformation of this fallen, disoriented, and distorted way of being. Understanding this fallen self is one of the important tasks in the process of spiritual formation. The battle with sin "rests on our ability to detect it, and then discipline ourselves against it."[8] Oswald Chambers wrote, "It is astounding how ignorant we are about ourselves!"[9] David Benner wrote similarly:

> The human capacity for self-deception is astounding. This is taught by Scripture (Jeremiah 17:9) and confirmed by psychology. Some people are highly skilled in deceiving others. However, their duplicity pales in comparison with the endlessly creative ways in which each and every one of us deceives our self.[10]

Like the addict who must first acknowledge addiction before the cure can begin, the fallen self must be acknowledged by the sinner for the Holy Spirit to accomplish the deep transformation we so badly need. Once acknowledged, a sinner can be led to understand the deep, hidden areas of his or her character through a gracious work of God. This was the pursuit of a group of monks who became known as the Desert Fathers. A young man named Anthony was among the first to sell his possessions and move into the Egyptian desert, cutting himself off from contact with the outside world. From around the year AD 270 and continuing for three hundred years, these monastics sought to combine a deep, sincere self-knowledge with a real experience of God. The Desert Fathers teach us a spirituality from below. They show us that we have to begin with ourselves and our passions. The way to God, for the Desert Fathers, always passes through self-knowledge. Evagrius Ponticus put it this way: "If you want to know God, learn to know yourself first!"[11]

We need to be very careful here. There is no room for justification by our works, no matter how good they may be. To avoid the error of justification by works, this statement of the Desert Fathers must be understood and applied as the perfection of the faith of a believer, not the believer's justification by grace through faith. In other words, we are not speaking of a non-believer coming to saving faith, but rather a believer seeking to be all Jesus saved him or her to be. Sanctification is the perfection of the faith of one who already believes. It finds expression in the desperate cry of the father who said to Jesus, "I do believe, but help me overcome my unbelief!" (Mark 9:24).

It is when we are able to ask the Holy Spirit to cleanse the deepest parts of our soul that our faith is true, living, and active. That is a sign of our love of God and our desire to please him:

> Therefore, we ask the Spirit to show us how our many spiritual hungers—for power, security, and comfort—drive us to sin. We ask God to show us how to feed these needs by filling us in new ways every day with Himself. In this way, we drive out the hungers that cause us to use other people wrongly and to fill our lives with worldly pursuits

and treasures that can never satisfy, because some set out on the path of Christ but remain captive to the empty cravings of the soul.[12]

Dallas Willard concluded that spiritual formation requires a "precise, testable, thorough knowledge of the human self."[13] Teresa of Avila said that no matter how high a state a soul may have attained, it never gets beyond the need for more self-knowledge.[14] The self is where we meet God and where the Holy Spirit is doing his work of transformation.

Great care must be taken to avoid self-centered introspection. This awareness of self is neither self-preoccupation nor psychoanalysis, nor is it an unhealthy introspection when pursued within the awareness of the love of God. It is not a self-help methodology that excludes grace but rather is a way of opening up to God's promise of more grace. This is not self-knowledge for its own sake. Rather, it is a gracious work of the Holy Spirit through which the believer joins in the journey of transformation. Michael W. Mangis, professor of psychology at Wheaton College, observed, "Self-awareness for its own sake brings little satisfaction. To know my heart is a start, but it leads nowhere if I cannot then open those newly discovered rooms to the light of God's transformation"[15] Self-knowledge has value to the extent it enables more effective surrender to the work of the Holy Spirit. The purpose of self-knowledge, then, lies in its usefulness as a means of promoting transformation by God's truth into his image.

So what has been said about the fallen self to this point? When God is not trusted as the Source of being, he has been replaced by the fallen self, which is inherently unable to provide true answers to intrinsic questions of life. These questions of life revolve around a need for a true sense of self-worth. Being human will naturally entail a need for self-worth, which will involve a search for identity, value (Who am I?), and meaning and purpose (Why am I here?). Reliance on the fallen self to provide answers to these basic questions can only result in distorted, self-serving answers. The Desert Fathers understood this, which led them to seek to identify basic tendencies of the fallen self, a search that led to the identification of the seven deadly sins—pride, anger, lust, envy, greed, gluttony, and sloth. Each of these is a sinful means by which the fallen self seeks to establish, maintain, and live out its false sense of self-worth. The Desert Fathers also identified the seven virtues—humility, patience, purity, brotherly love, generosity, perseverance, and abstinence. These are ways in which we love God and others, and are examined in detail in the next book, *The Quest for Holiness—From Deadly Sin to Divine Virtue.*

Thus, the battle with the fallen self is a battle over the means of satisfying natural desires that are God-given. The image of God does not envision the elimination of these natural desires as some Eastern religions would promote. Rather, the need of the fallen self is one of transformation, or reorientation, of the self:

> Natural desires are those tendencies or inclinations that are part of our humanity. They are neither good nor evil, and they will stay with us from the cradle to the grave no matter what

progress we make toward sanctification. These are the basic needs of security, significance, love and acceptance, intimacy, and the like. To deny these is not to be sanctified, but detached from the rest of humanity. To pray they vanish is to pray in vain, for God will never take away by grace what he gave us by nature. Everyone has these desires, sinner or saint. We need to purify the means by which we satisfy them. For instance we will be tempted to satisfy the natural desire for security with evil desires of materialism or stinginess. We are tempted to fulfill the natural desire for significance through pride and power. We may be tempted to gratify our wholesome need for love and acceptance through promiscuity. In any case, our real enemy here is not the natural desire, but the evil desires which flow from it.[16]

This is an important distinction. God-given desires will never be sinful but can be satisfied through sinful means. The temptation to satisfy God-given desires through selfish means will always be present, but from our knowledge of the fallen self comes the ability to test our natural inclinations against mature values such as the last shall be first, the forgiveness of others, confession of sin, and love of neighbor. As we followers of Jesus know ourselves and understand and acknowledge the consequence of the fall more deeply, we gain the ability to more fully surrender to and participate in the life-transforming work of the Holy Spirit.

When we follow Jesus in discipleship, Jesus' way of being identified by the Father becomes ingrained in our lives. In other words, in and through faith we find that our true identity lies in our intimate relation to God. We understand more and more deeply that we are in our design and in our fulfillment children of God, which is a return to the intimacy of the garden of Eden. The source upon which we rely for our identity is shifted from the fallen self to God:

> The intensity of the Spirit's convicting negation of our reliance on the ego to hold on to and protect our identity is truly gracious. This illuminative experience expands our intentionality, our way of interpreting the world. Resting in the infinite faithfulness of the divine Spirit, we are opened up into new life—receiving our identity as we are bound together with Christ in relation to God. This gracious constitution of the self liberates us from the tension of an ego-centric life. The human spirit comes to rest in the infinite Power that holds it together and calls it into a share in the intimacy of divine life. This spiritual union with God involves sharing in the knowledge of Jesus Christ, *who laid down his life in order to take it up again in utter dependence on the Father* (John 10:17–18). The same Spirit that raised Christ from the dead dwells in us (Romans 8:11) so that we may now become wise as we learn to lay down our ego functions as the ground of our identity, taking them up again only as we live in faithfulness to the Son of God (Galatians 2:20).

The intensification of faith—our being bound
in and to the absolute mutual fidelity that is the
divine life—enables us to lose our lives in order
to find them truly in the Spirit (Matthew 10:39;
16:25). (emphasis added)[17]

In this action of Jesus of laying down his life and
taking it up in utter dependence on the Father, the creative
design of trust is manifestly present. Here is the ultimate
example of trust in God, a quality of the image of God in
which we were created.

In his letter to the Philippians, Paul provided an
instance of the reordering of this drive within that
occurs through spiritual formation. In that letter Paul
wrote that he had learned to be content in all things
(Philippians 4:11). He could write this statement even
though he was locked in a Roman prison. Yet he was
confident he would be delivered, not from prison but
from any shame that might result from a failure of his life
to exalt Jesus. It is this understanding, this confidence, this
trust, that allowed him to say, "For to me, living means
living for Christ, and dying is even better" (Phil. 1:21).
Paul was still motivated to achieve those things that were
the priorities of his life, but as Paul had learned to live
in the Spirit, those priorities had been reordered. He had
been transformed from a legalistic Pharisee bent on the
destruction of the church to a man with the desire to live
for Jesus and exalt him (God), and to love and serve the
church (others). Paul was transformed from achieving his
own self-centered goals by his own means to glorifying
God by whatever means God chose for him.

What are the desires upon which our hearts are set? For many years I read Psalm 37:4 to mean that if I did my part in my relationship with God then God would give me what *I* wanted. "Take delight in the LORD, and he will give you your heart's desires." I have come to see a different, more meaningful interpretation of this passage. I now read the psalm to say that as my relationship with God grows, he will put his desires in my heart. In other words, this is not a passage about what I want, but rather about the opening of my heart so that what God wants becomes what I want. Spiritual formation in Christ moves toward a total interchange of our desires for his desires.

What is it that we really desire? What we truly desire, what we are most passionate about, will determine how we organize our lives. Paul encouraged the Philippians to pattern their lives after him (Philippians 3:17). He encouraged believers not to worry but rather to pray and trust God for their provision. That is the design found in creation, the image of God. It is an image that reflects the interdependence within the Holy Trinity, which we can see most clearly in the dependence of Jesus upon the Father. But how is this possible? A little phrase added by Paul provides an understanding of reality that captures the meaning of this reorientation: "Remember, the Lord is coming soon" (Phil. 4:5). Paul urged the Philippians to orient their lives around the truth of the return of Jesus. He said essentially the same thing when he said, "But we are citizens of heaven, where the Lord Jesus Christ lives" (Phil. 3:20). Live according to a reality that transcends this temporary life. This is a reality beyond what can be perceived with our senses. It is a reality promised by God and accepted by faith. With the return of Jesus will come the final victory. But this is not just a future coming. We dwell within this reality here and now. When our lives are oriented around this return and this victory, we are motivated, indeed empowered, to trust deeply in the ultimate provision of God for all things and to live accordingly. We are thirsty for God and we are invited to drink deeply (Psalm 42:2). This reality is the foundation for the joy which Paul also urged in this letter; "Always be full of joy in the Lord, I say it again—rejoice!" (Phil. 4:4). Joy is a Romans 8:28 outlook on life.

Reflection and Application

1. The fallen self is presented in contrast with the self as created by God. Describe the changes that occurred as a result of the decision of Adam and Eve to disobey the command of God, in other words, to sin? What does this add to what we understand is meant when we say our relationship with God was broken?

2. Read the following passages carefully: Romans 3:23; 7:21–23; Hebrews 12:1. What do they tell us about sin and the influence sin has over us?

3. Michael Mangis said this about the verse in Hebrews:

> No matter how it is worded, the phrase suggests a type of sin with a quality of such nearness that we forget it is there. I picture something like spandex. I don't notice it until I take a step and it pulls me in the wrong direction and causes me to stumble. Jesus used the analogy of yeast in bread dough. Sin suffuses itself throughout our beings and cannot be separated from the other ingredients.[18]

How does this influence your understanding of sin? Is sin only what someone does or is there a more pervasive quality to sin? Can God help us with all aspects of sin in our lives?

4. The idea presented in this chapter is that in our spiritual formation we should seek to know both God and ourselves. Self-knowledge is a tool which we can use

as we seek to open ourselves to the transforming truth revealed in Jesus. What do you hear that is helpful in this idea? What danger might there be in this idea? We read that Dallas Willard said a precise, testable, thorough knowledge of self is necessary in our spiritual formation. What are some areas in which you might grow in self-knowledge?

5. Instructions we are to follow include the last shall be first, the forgiveness of others, and love of neighbor. What are some everyday ways in which self-knowledge may help you open your life in response to these instructions? How will you practice these in your life? Write out a prayer that might result from self-knowledge with regard to one or more of these commands.

4

Called to Holiness: The Hope of Spiritual Formation

Holiness is not merely the changing of our status in heaven; it is acknowledging our love for God and our desire to look more and more like him, whom we say we love. It is an ever-increasing oneness prompted by love.

—STEVE DENEFF

The message Jesus and his disciples taught to and through the early church was not only a message of forgiveness. It was not only a message of a judicial restoration of one's relationship with God. It was a message of newness of life, transformation of life, here and now. Paul preached that the gospel message possesses the potential for real change in people and their personalities, such that we are able to vividly and compellingly see a life that is an alternative to one dominated by sin.[1] This means real, present transformation, a transformation into greater and greater Christlikeness, into the image of God, and into holiness. It comes as a command of God, a call to holiness, and is to be known and experienced as a dynamic reality in the everyday life of every follower of Jesus.

47

It is hardly deniable that Scripture issues a call to holiness given the command of the Father (Leviticus 19:2), of the Son (Matthew 5:48), and of the Holy Spirit by the inspiration given to Peter (1 Peter 1:15–16). In the midst of giving the law to the Israelites, the Father commanded, "You must be holy because I, the LORD your God, am holy" (Lev. 19:2). When teaching the disciples what it means to live as true children of the Father, Jesus commanded, "But you are to be perfect, even as your Father in heaven is perfect" (Matt. 5:48). Under the inspiration of the Holy Spirit, Peter wrote to the dispersed church, urging them to live as obedient children and reminding them, "But now you must be holy in everything you do, just as God who chose you is holy. For the Scriptures say, 'You must be holy because I am holy'" (1 Peter 1:15–16). The call to holiness is Trinitarian, and growth in holiness involves Trinitarian action in the believer, the will of the Father, the example of the Son, and the indwelling of the Holy Spirit.[2]

The fact that it is Trinitarian adds great emphasis to this call to holiness. The question is how are we going to respond? It's so easy to read some of the standards in the Bible and think, *That sounds nice; it might be good for a monk or a preacher, but I could never be that kind of person.* Yet, we are told without equivocation that we are to love God with all our heart, to love our neighbor, and to be holy. The Bible is not a book that sets out high and lofty ideals that are appealing but can be ignored because they are impossible to obtain. It is a practical book of life, not because we are able to live it out but precisely because its demands upon us come with the power of God helping us respond. But we immediately encounter a problem if we think of holiness as something to be achieved, a box to be checked, or a task to be completed. Holiness is not simply about keeping a list of things we do and don't do. Sure, that is part of it, but holiness is much more. Holiness is about our total relationship with God. "Sin is, at its root, the absence of God. Holiness, at its root, is the presence of God."[3] When we looked at the sin of Adam and Eve, we noted that they chose a situation in which the manifest presence of God was absent. An inseparable part of their sin was their choice of life in the absence of God. Holiness "is ultimately about the full manifestation of God's presence with His people. This is why the essence of sin is choosing the absence of God. In contrast, holiness, at its very foundation, is the sign and seal of God's presence in the world."[4]

The holiness of God is perfect and unchanging. The follower of Jesus experiences holiness as being set apart or consecrated for the purposes of God and growth in the likeness of Christ. It is a high calling, indeed the highest calling, in a believer's life and hence has immediate and profound meaning to a believer:

> [H]oliness is not merely the changing of our status in heaven; it is acknowledging our love for God and our desire *to look more and more like him*, whom we say we love. It is *an ever-increasing oneness* prompted by love. In our conversion, we were driven or pushed into repentance by a deep conviction or guilt over having broken the rules (Galatians 3:24). In sanctification, we are pulled

or compelled by a holy fascination to become
one again with the Father and to bear his image.
(emphasis added)[5]

Holiness is a reorientation of our life to the created order
of relationship found in the garden of Eden. Relationship
is key!

A life of holiness is somehow instinctively understood
as standing in opposition to a life that conforms to the
destructive and dehumanizing standards of the world. It
is a life that is moral, sacred, and pure, standing in opposition to that which is profane, godless, and irreverent. We
read of the transition between these two ways of living in
the words of Scripture: "My old self has been crucified
with Christ. It is no longer I who live, but Christ lives in
me" (Gal. 2:20) and "For you died to this life, and your real
life is hidden with Christ in God" (Col. 3:3). The regeneration that comes through the gospel is freedom from
the power of sin, the freedom to live life as God intended,
life measured by holiness (Romans 8:2).

Questions regarding this regeneration, of the moral
character of the believer after the new birth, have challenged theologians since the days of the early church fathers.
A person is sinful before salvation, and a transformation
occurs when Jesus is accepted as Savior. There is general
agreement among Christians that this is true, but it is also
the source of disagreement. Specifically, the extent of this
transformation has been and remains a point of difference
even among evangelical perspectives. This is the subject of
Five Views on Sanctification, a book that brings together
major Protestant views on what it means to live a holy, or

sanctified life. Nuances in the theology of sanctification come from Wesleyan, Reformed, Pentecostal, Keswick, and Augustinian-Dispensational camps. However, more revealing than the extent of disagreement is the recognition of the extent of agreement. "While in every perspective there may be those who will go to extremes that contradict the mainstream of their perspective, when conservative and sober judgment is applied, it is remarkable how similar the various views on sanctification are."[6] Today when there is such a great need for unity within the church, it is worth accentuating this depth of agreement. Still, there is benefit from an awareness of these differing views.

If sin is disobedience and dishonor of God, holiness is obedience that glorifies God. Among various doctrinal positions within the Christian faith, general agreement is found in the promise of victory over sin to every disciple of Jesus. Consider these statements regarding five distinct doctrinal positions. The Wesleyan view states, "Every person who is born of God, from the moment of regeneration, has the promise of victory over sin and the devil and has the power of the Holy Spirit to realize that victory in everyday living."[7] The Reformed position is that, "Sanctification empowers us to think, will, and love in a way that glorifies God, namely, to think God's thoughts after Him and to do what is in harmony with His will."[8] For the Keswick position on victory over sin it has been said, "The *normal* Christian life is one of uniform sustained victory over known sin; and that no temptation is permitted to happen to us without a way of escape being provided by God"[9] (1 Cor. 10:13). The Pentecostal perspective holds that "sanctification enables us to live above the sin, self-will, and spiritual anarchy of the world and to live for God instead."[10] The Augustinian-Dispensational perspective might be captured in this statement: "Although the old nature is present, by the power of the Spirit the new nature can be enabled to manifest the fruit of the Spirit, namely, 'love, joy, peace, patience, kindness, goodness, faithfulness, gentleness and self-control' (Gal. 5:22–23)."[11] Each of these position statements contains an acknowledgment of empowerment of the believer by grace for victory over sin. Each recognizes the possibility of transformation from a life lived to serve and satisfy our own distorted purposes to a life lived to glorify God.

In each of these evangelical perspectives we find a work of the Holy Spirit that occurs in a moment and a progressive component in sanctification. It is obvious that growth in holiness must have a point of beginning, and while it may be experienced differently, that beginning is no insignificant moment. It in some way must involve a glimpse of the holiness of God that leaves an awareness in the believer that he or she is not holy and is dependent for change upon the grace of God. This illumination is one form of the power of the gospel, the impact of this awareness showing us who we are and who we are called to become. It enables us to see and be called by a compelling vision of life as God intended it to be. This moment has the potential of radical transformation, the beginning of a life reoriented from self to God and realigned with God's purposes.

While the process begins in a moment in time, it is not completed in that initial desire for the holiness of God. But there can be a reorientation. We can experience a change in which we no longer think longingly of the old life when the true desire of our heart is to be nearer and nearer to God, more like Jesus, and growing steadily in holiness. It is "a journey involving many exciting, and sometimes agonizing, discoveries. It is a passing from unconscious depravity to conscious depravity, commenced by learning that we know not."[12] The follower of Jesus no longer turns from sin with regret but instead knows joy in seeking to be more like Jesus. Dallas Willard wrote of this reorientation:

> The overall orientation of their will, the kinds of thoughts and feelings that occupy them, the "automatic" inclinations and "readinesses" of their body in action, the prevailing posture of their relations toward others, and the harmonious wholeness of their soul—these all, through the formative processes undergone by his disciples, *increasingly come to resemble the personal dimensions of their Master.* (emphasis added)[13]

Each tradition has the restoration of the image of God, and in some sense its fulfillment, in view, but the extent to which this restoration occurs is the point of greatest disagreement. Stanley Horton framed the issue this way: "Since this aspect of sanctification is progressive, the question becomes: How far can we progress? Or what degree of perfection can we attain in this life?"[14] While these positions will never be precisely the same, there is a remarkable similarity in viewpoints as the consideration moves beyond the ultimate language of perfection and on to consideration of the implementation of these perspectives. Melvin Dieter further explained the Wesleyan perspective by stating, "It is a life, not of any kind of sinless perfection, but of being enabled by the grace of God not to sin."[15] Again, able to stand, yet living life with the potential of falling into sin. Although the Reformed tradition rejects the use of "perfection," Anthony Hoekema wrote, "Sanctification empowers us to think, will, and love in a way that glorifies God, namely, to think God's thoughts after Him and to do what is in harmony with His will."[16] A life lived in this manner has been remarkably transformed. The Keswick view brings the gracious gift of the mind of Christ into awareness (1 Corinthians 2:16):

> The normal Christian overcomes in the battle with temptation, consistently obeys the laws of God, and grows in self-control, contentment, humility, and courage. Thought processes are so under the control of the Holy Spirit and instructed by Scripture that the normal Christian authentically reflects the attitudes and behavior of Jesus Christ. *God has first place in life, and the welfare of others takes precedence over personal desires.* (emphasis added)[17]

Surely the Pentecostal position has much in common with the Wesleyan and the Reformed positions when it is characterized as "the whole-hearted desire and determination to do the will of God."[18] The focus is on perfection of the desire not the realization or perfect implementation of that desire. "For God is working in you, giving you the desire and the power to do what pleases him" (Phil. 2:13).

Noting that the fruit of the Spirit comes from "the Spirit of God using the human body," the Augustinian-Dispensational perspective allows that "[i]n this sense the believer can be Christlike, even in this life."[19] Of course, to be Christlike is to be holy, restored to the image of God. All five perspectives speak of newness of life, victory over sin, and an empowerment that comes through the Holy Spirit. To this I would add that there is no limit to the work that might be done by the omnipotent, indwelling Holy Spirit.

In these days it is all too commonly heard, "I'm a sinner and I'm going to sin every day." As an acknowledgment that the process of sanctification is not complete and will not be completed in this life, perhaps this conveys some truth. But we must keep in mind that this statement is heard by a population in which the vast majority has little thought about moving into a full relationship with Jesus. Given the state of the church today, such a statement is more likely to lead people to error and apathy. It is too easy to add to this statement, "So nothing can be done about it and I'm just going to keep on sinning." There is a widespread conviction in the world and even in the church that *sin wins*. The admonitions of the apostle Paul expressed precisely the opposite: promise of victory *over* sin, not the victory *of* sin. Believing that we are fundamentally helpless sinners without the power of the indwelling Holy Spirit can only lead to failure. James Byron Smith quoted David C. Needham in his book, "What could be more frustrating than being a Christian who thinks himself to be primarily a self-centered sinner, yet whose purpose in life is to produce God-centered holiness?"[20]

Let's return to the notion that we can live with whole-hearted desire and determination to do the will of God. Think of a child giving a gift of love to a parent. The gift may be flawed in some way. The freshly picked bouquet of flowers for Mom may actually have come from the neighbor's garden, or the cool glass of water for Dad may be served in a dirty glass, but the desire of the child's heart is grounded in love. We find holiness in this perfect desire. Only Jesus lived life in perfect humility, perfect patience, perfect brotherhood, perfect purity, and so on. For the rest of us, many of our best actions may be tainted in some way by self-centeredness. Yet, we can find holiness in our perfect desires. We can continue to grow in holiness by God's grace, but the presence of holiness is found in relationship with God, not a record of how we succeeded or failed in keeping a list of dos and don'ts. There are two extremes among people responding to the command to be holy: those who say they can never be holy and those who say they live in sinless perfection. What we need to ask of ourselves is whether our lives reflect a growing relationship of love of God and love of neighbor. What is God asking of us? He is not looking so much for holiness in doing as for holiness in being. Of course, holiness in being is going to result more and more in holiness of doing.

This comparative analysis of these evangelical positions points to common ground among these doctrines and gives us a deeper understanding of what the Christian faith has come to believe the call to holiness to mean. One commonly held belief is that all Christians are confronted by a Trinitarian call to holy living. The power for holy living is also graciously Trinitarian, but especially associated with the indwelling Holy Spirit. The disciple of Jesus is given the promise of being empowered to live a life dedicated to God with victory over sin, grows throughout this life in Christlikeness, and can live a life that pleases and glorifies God. But it must be said again, this is not just living by a list of dos and don'ts. It is a relationship where our hearts want for ourselves, our families, our community, and our world what God wants for us. It is a deepening trust in whatever context we may find ourselves that God is sovereign, good, and holy.

These traditions all maintain a serious view of sin and its destructive consequences. From these statements of doctrine, none can be charged with the heresy of a lax attitude toward sin. Perhaps common ground is also found in answer to the question, "What sin is excusable?" All traditions would answer that believers can have victory over any temptation and there is no sin that may be excused. Each and every sin is one for which Jesus died on the cross. Indeed, all would say that disciples of Jesus have been freed from the domination of sin and are empowered to grow in the holiness of God. The call to such a life is, indeed, a high calling.

Reflection and Application

1. Definition of *holy*: set apart or consecrated to God. The principal terms that are translated "holy" in English are *kadosh* (Hebrew) and *hagios* (Greek). Other words that come from the same roots are: sanctify, sanctification, and "hallowed" (or "holy-ed"). Other terms that often occur in conjunction or parallel with holy include: perfect, irreproachable, blameless, and pure.

2. Read: Leviticus 19:2; Matthew 5:48; 1 Peter 1:16.
   Reinforce your understanding of holiness through these passages:

   • Who is issuing the command?
   • What do you like when you read these passages?
   • What do you dislike when you read these passages?
   • How do you *feel* when you read these texts?
   • What happens when you add the other words or phrases listed above to these?

3. Reflect on the idea of holiness of doing and holiness of being. How would you explain these two attributes to someone trying to understand holiness? Can you pursue holiness of doing and exclude holiness of being? Can you pursue holiness of being and exclude holiness of doing?

4. Interested in digging a little deeper? In the Old Testament, holiness was often used to speak of position in relation to God rather than a condition of the heart (Exodus 19:6; 30:29; Ezekiel 37:28). In the New

Testament, holiness is seen as conformity to the nature of God. Sometimes this conformity is a work that God has completed (imputed holiness), and sometimes it is a work that God is doing (imparted holiness). Look for the difference in the following verses and note what they say about holiness:

Romans 6:19	Ephesians 1:4
Romans 12:1–2	Ephesians 4:12–13
1 Corinthians 6:11	Ephesians 4:21–24
2 Corinthians 3:18	1 Thessalonians 4:3
Hebrews 10:14	1 Thessalonians 5:23
Hebrews 12:14	2 Peter 3:14

5. Take time to compose a prayer about holiness. What would you like God to do in your life? What is the desire of your heart for understanding, commitment, or transformation?

5

Transformation: The Work of the Holy Spirit

Lord, how absolutely necessary to me is Your grace if I want to begin something good, to continue with it, and then to complete it. Without Your grace I can do nothing, but with it strengthening me I can do all things.

—Thomas à Kempis

We have observed that the call to holiness is a Trinitarian call. It reflects the will of the Father, the obedient life of the Son, and the work of the Holy Spirit. It is with awe for this Source of the Christian life that Paul admonished the believer to work out his or her salvation with deep reverence and fear of God (Philippians 2:12). In urging us to work out our salvation, Paul implied that there is something more that we need to know about salvation than might appear at first blush. We are saved by grace through faith, not by works (Ephesians 2:8). We must come to know this, at least implicitly, when we first make a confession of faith in Jesus as our Savior. In saying we are to work out our salvation, was Paul creating a conflict? Of course not! He was helping us understand that our salvation begins with justification, continues with sanctification, and ascends to glorification at death. The transformation that Paul envisioned is the real promise of spiritual formation—the completeness of the gift of salvation—but it brings to the follower of Jesus a dilemma. The problem with this command is that a person, regardless of what they may do, cannot make himself or herself holy.

Willpower has been the focus of much research. It has been defined as the ability to resist short-term gratification in order to achieve long-term goals.[1] Another name for willpower is self-control, an appropriate title given that the self is a primary topic in this book.

Transformation of the heart into one of inner righteousness cannot be brought about by willpower and determination. That is not to say willpower is not important, but it is not enough for transformation at the deepest level of our spirit. Rather, reliance is placed on the inner working of God for such transformation, a belief that distinguishes the Christian faith from the many works-based religions. Oswald Chambers, in his devotional *My Utmost for His Highest*, put it like this:

> If Jesus Christ is going to regenerate me, what is the problem He faces? It is simply this—I have a heredity in which I had no say or decision; I am not holy, nor am I likely to be; and if all Jesus Christ can do is tell me that I must be holy, His teaching only causes me to despair. But if Jesus Christ is truly a regenerator, someone who can put His own heredity of holiness into me, then I can begin to see what He means when He says

that I have to be holy. Redemption means that Jesus Christ can put into anyone the hereditary nature that was in Himself.[2]

Chambers understood that our Christian faith is not so much about our disciplined pursuit of God as it is God's relentless pursuit of us. He sees the impossibility of the command to be holy if it is to be achieved by the self-effort of the believer. The solution is in the sharing of the nature of Jesus. Such a radical change can only be accomplished by God, specifically through the indwelling work of the Holy Spirit. "The great, mysterious work of the Holy Spirit is in the deep recesses of our being which we cannot reach. . . . The same Spirit that fed the life of Jesus Christ will feed the life of our spirit."[3] The Holy Spirit directs our lives and shows us truth with the single aim of making us disciples of Jesus. It is not contradictory to speak of this as being accomplished through the work of the Holy Spirit. While the sanctification of a follower of Jesus does involve all the persons of the Trinity, the work of the Holy Spirit occupies a position of prominence in this aspect of Trinitarian work:

Because our understanding of the transforma-tion of the creaturely *human* spirit will be shaped (whether consciously or not) by our understanding of the creative *divine* Spirit, one of the most relevant theological themes for understanding spirituality is Pneumatology—the doctrine of the Holy Spirit. Given its implicit significance, it is initially surprising that so many popular Christian treatments of spirituality do not embed

their presentations within an articulation of the
doctrine of the Holy Spirit.[4]

In other words, our understanding of and submission
to the transformation of our spirit is strengthened as we
come to a deeper understanding of the work of the Holy
Spirit. Any effective effort at spiritual formation, whether
individual or corporate, must be pursued in an atmo-
sphere that allows for the working of the Holy Spirit. We
remember, of course, that the end result of the work of the
Holy Spirit is that the will of the Father may be done and
the Father and the Son may be glorified.

The Holy Spirit has been working since the beginning. The Old Testament prophets Jeremiah and Ezekiel
knew something of the natural condition of the human
heart. They knew it to be deceitful and desperately wicked
(Jeremiah 17:9), hard as stone in its attitude toward God,
and disobedient (Ezekiel 11:19). They also knew the
remedy for this flawed heart, a remedy which comes not
from within by works, but from outside of us by grace.
Indeed, they heard God's promise of a new spirit and a
tender heart that would make obedience to God possible.
They understood that God was promising to put his Spirit
in men and women in a way that they might obey his
commands (Ezekiel 36:27).

The promise known by these Old Testament
prophets was forward-looking. While the promise was
realized in special circumstance in Old Testament times,
its greater realization awaited the resurrection of Jesus
when the Holy Spirit was given to all who believed in
him (John 7:39). Jesus saw this full giving of the Spirit as

an important consequence of his resurrection and ascension. As the second person of the Trinity, he promised the disciples that if they asked the Father, he would give the Holy Spirit, a promise whose fulfillment began on the day of Pentecost (Acts 2:4). The outpouring of the Holy Spirit at Pentecost was a pivotal point in the history of the church. At that point the focus changed from the finished work of Jesus on the cross to include the ongoing work of the Holy Spirit: "In Christ, we speak chiefly of 'God for us.' Now we speak more purposely of 'God working in us.'"[5] That is the role of the Holy Spirit.

This does not in any way set aside or minimize the atoning work of Jesus. It is still and always will be on the basis of that work that Jesus said, "No one can come to the Father except through me" (John 14:6). Nor does this in any way suggest that Jesus is not at work in the world, especially in the lives of believers. He is constantly interceding and sustaining, and the work of his gracious love is unending. But the precise work of the Holy Spirit is to indwell the believer, thereby meeting him or her at the very point where transformation is desperately needed, the fallen self.

The Holy Spirit is referred to as *holy* because the specific work of the third person of the Trinity is the work of sanctification. The Holy Spirit is a *sanctifying* Spirit. The work of sanctification is always at the initiative of God and God alone. Thomas à Kempis wrote, "Lord, how absolutely necessary to me is Your grace if I want to begin something good, to continue with it, and then to complete it. Without Your grace I can do nothing, but with it strengthening me I can do all things."[6]

One means of God's grace is the work of the Holy Spirit. The essential, initiating, and empowering "work of the Holy Spirit is the most distinctive aspect of Christian formation in contrast to every other form of secular spirituality that usually draws strength from human psyche or spiritual forces."[7]

The question that now begs to be answered is how the Holy Spirit accomplishes this work. The work of the Holy Spirit is beyond our full understanding and will be experienced in many different ways. Yet it was nothing less than the promise of Jesus to the disciples that he would ask the Father who would send the Holy Spirit (John 14:16; 15:26). The Holy Spirit is the One who would lead them into all truth (John 14:17; 16:13). This truth certainly has an intellectual component, but its reference is primarily relational truth. It is about true personhood, the truth of what it means to be a person created in the image of God and living as a disciple of Jesus. It is truth that will guide the believer into a life "liberated from the painful relations of sin and into the peaceful relationship of fellowship with God and neighbor."[8]

The work of the Holy Spirit may also be seen specifically in teaching the believers (John 14:26), convincing the world of sin and God's righteousness (John 16:8), helping in distress (1 Peter 4:14), and praying for believers (Romans 8:26), while in all things bringing glory to Jesus (John 16:14). Perhaps most crucial, though, is the work of illumination of the gospel, enabling believers to understand and accept the Word, and inspiring the believer through the Word.[9] "The Holy Spirit teaches and admonishes us when we read Scripture. He gives us the gift of discernment so that we might have the mind of Christ and to think about things in ways that are informed by godly wisdom."[10] There is a supernatural aspect to this work that is beyond our comprehension (Isaiah 55:8–9). There is also this aspect of illumination, an awareness of sin and of the possibility of an alternative life that is not dominated by sin. For a person who believes in God, heaven, and hell, it is easy to see the desirability of a life headed to heaven over a life headed to hell. For a person who has the promise of heaven, it is more difficult to see the desirability of a life lived in submission to holiness versus a life surrendered to the false promises of the world. By grace we are enabled to see what a life looks like if it is dominated by relationship with God. The Holy Spirit works by "making the gospel dynamic and transforming in cultures, centuries, people and situations that are quite different from the first-century context."[11] Illuminated by the Holy Spirit, Scripture becomes a means of God's grace, that is, a means through which God's grace is extended to humankind.

Believers are urged to follow the Spirit rather than their sinful nature (Romans 8:4), indeed, to be controlled by the Spirit (Romans 8:6). To use Paul's words, the Holy Spirit writes the law on believers' hearts, the law of the love of God and the love of neighbor. If the fall resulted in the introduction of an active power that predisposes our hearts toward sin and disobedience, the Holy Spirit is an active power and initiates active inward processes turning the hearts of believers back toward God.

The Old Testament writers came to realize that the fallen nature involves the human spirit—that which motivates, forms attitudes, and promotes behavior. The quickening of the spiritual senses is a work of the Holy Spirit on our spirits: "In quickening the soul, God brings its senses to life, such that they perceive the spiritual realm in general and the divine love in particular."[12] This quickening of the senses allows new perspectives, motivations, and desires. "Sin almost always presents itself to us as something alluring, attractive, desirable, as something that will give power to our lives."[13] The Holy Spirit enables the believer to distinguish between truth and lie, and to see an alternative, true life:

> It is for want of the greater vision, for want of knowing the one thing we are here to do, that all other things become more appealing. But once the grace of God appears—once our imaginations have been arrested by the image of Jesus—we know at once why we are here and all other pursuits and pleasures are put in their context and kept in their proportion.[14]

Wesley referred to what results as "a change from unholy tempers or dispositions to holy ones, from pride to humility, from passion to meekness, from peevishness and discontent to patience and resignation."[15] The seeds of holy desires and attitudes are implanted in the soul. These are the seeds of holiness.

Every believer is called by God to imitate Jesus and be restored to his image. The beauty of this call is that he provides the power to make significant progress in that direction. This explains why the work of the Holy Spirit is frequently referred to as a power for change of our sinful nature (Romans 8:2; Philippians 2:13; Ephesians 3:16).

Believers are given a new spirit and changed "from a stub-born 'I'-centered response to a malleable, God-centered one"[16] and the Holy Spirit is the Source through which this gift of a new spirit is given. The Holy Spirit will lead the believer to see that the worldly pursuits that seem appealing but are contrary to God's will really are not in his or her best interest. When the promised fulfillment of a life in Christ is revealed, a person is enabled, empowered, and motivated to turn away from those things shown to be deceptive, destructive, dehumanizing, and temporal in order to seize the prize of eternal life, a life lived according to the design of its Creator.

We can think of the work of the Holy Spirit as the reversal of the consequences of the fall and restoration of intimate relationship with God. This work began when God returned to the garden of Eden and sought out Adam and Eve (Genesis 3:9). This work includes guiding and molding the believer into a nature that increasingly finds delight in responding to the Holy Spirit, a life of joyful surrender such as that lived by Jesus. Oswald Chambers wrote:

> Sanctification means being made one with Jesus so that the nature that controlled Him will control us. Are we really prepared for what that will cost? It will cost absolutely everything in us which is not of God. . . . Are we prepared to say, "Lord, make me, a sinner saved by grace, as holy as You can"? Jesus prayed that we might be one with Him, just as He is one with the Father.[17]

The ways of God are far beyond our full under-standing (Isaiah 55:8–9). His work in our lives includes "the profound truth that goes beyond forgiveness . . . that God is trying to give his nature to us."[18] The nature of Jesus was sinless obedience to the Father. Jesus understood with every fiber of his being that the Father is good and that obedience to his perfect will is an embrace of perfect truth.

As believers, we are new persons (2 Corinthians 5:17). Where the desire of the old nature was to serve self, in the believer the Holy Spirit causes our spirit to desire to submit to God's will (Philippians 2:13). This is a deep transformation of the heart, but one that few followers of Jesus seek or experience.[19] This desire is for Christlikeness, the restoration of the image of God in the disciple of Jesus. Clearly the breadth and depth of change brought by the Holy Spirit impacts the entire life of the believer. Change of the *religious life*, what is done on Sundays, during devotions, and at Bible studies, is not enough. The common life must be surrendered to change as well, which includes how we treat our spouse and children, the way we drive our cars, and the messages we take in through our senses. Every feature of one's life will experience change when we are being led by the Holy Spirit into the image of Christ.

To speak of the work of the Holy Spirit is to speak of a continuous, gracious intervention in our life. Throughout our life, the Holy Spirit is "regenerating and conforming us to the image of Jesus Christ as the Spirit indwells, fills, guides, gifts, and empowers people for life in the community of faith and in the world."[20] To be recreated in the image of God is to be recreated in true personhood, something lost in the fall. True personhood has a true center, and God is that center. The result of the fall was that the fallen self was placed at the center of one's existence. That means that the satisfaction of the desires of self—desires that often are not aligned with the goodness of God—guides our life. With the working out of our salvation comes knowledge of an alternative life that the new believer knows is more desirable, or at least perceives is more true. "There is a desire that comes from a regenerated person—all things have become new, including the desire to please God and to prove His perfect will (see 2 Corinthians 5:17)."[21]

The Holy Spirit convicts, convinces, calls, and loves a person into a desire to know and be known by God. This unique character of Christian spiritual formation is this yearning for a closer relationship with God. This yearning must have been burning in the heart of the psalmist when he wrote, "As a deer longs for flowing streams, so my soul longs for you, O God. My soul thirsts for God, for the living God. When shall I come and behold the face of God?" (Psalms 42:1–2 NRSV). Spiritual formation is the working out of this yearning, this gift of salvation, into greater and greater fullness. Though we are not told with certainty, we might imagine that this yearning was satisfied for Adam and Eve before they chose the absence of God, and all of us as their descendants have been seeking satisfaction of this yearning ever since.

The emerging desire that comes with this transformation is tantamount to saying that the sanctification brought into the life of the believer is a change in identity. This change of identity is a change in the essence, the very being, of the believer. In terms of the temptation of Adam and Eve, this change of identity is from one who places trust in oneself to one who has a deep and growing trust in God. Eve did not understand or did not accept that God created her to rest in the assurance of his salvation. The offer from God was a rest envisioned by the psalmist when he wrote, "But I have calmed and quieted my soul, like a weaned child with its mother; my soul is like the weaned child that is with me" (Psalms 131:2 NRSV). We can almost feel a sense of peace and contentment in the psalmist's words. When faced with temptation, Eve concluded that she had to disobey God to get what she thought she needed, what she wanted, or what she deserved. She did not trust God's command to be the very best for her, and this attitude of distrust prevented her rest in God. Jesus, on the other hand, modeled an unwavering trust in the Father for those who follow him:

> As we find our identity mediated by the presence of the eternal Spirit, our way of knowing and being-known is transformed; our desire for wisdom takes shape as an identification with the reconciling faithfulness of God in the world. . . . [T]his means that the Christian experience of becoming wise involves participating in Jesus Christ's trusting of the Father in the Spirit.[22]

Fallen humanity continues to resist trusting God for the satisfaction of its deepest needs, trusting instead in its own ability to find peace, contentment, and rest. In response, God sent his Son. This ultimate act of love is the measure of the extent to which God may be trusted. Believers are saved by that death and are charged to work out their salvation (Philippians 2:12). The Holy Spirit leads people in this salvation into deeper and deeper surrender as they accept deep in their hearts that God truly loves them and can be trusted with their lives. The Holy Spirit causes our hearts to sing "I love you" back to the Lord.

Reflection and Application

1. Anchor the work of the Holy Spirit in a biblical foundation by looking up these passages and answering the questions that follow:

   - John 14:26; 16:13; Romans 8:4–9, 26; Ephesians 3:16; 1 Corinthians 2:16
   - What are the ways in which the Holy Spirit is said to work?
   - How is this a work that brings Christlikeness to the believer or restores the image of God in the believer?
   - What would you add to this list from other Scripture?

2. Are you at ease with the work of the Holy Spirit in your life? What can you do in your life to make more room for this work of the Holy Spirit? Remember, this is a process that continues through all of your life.

3. Compose a prayer listing and thanking God for specific ways the Holy Spirit has worked in your life.

   > Clearly, the breadth of change is the entire life of the believer. It's not enough to change our religious life, what we do on Sundays, during devotions and at Bible studies. We must surrender to change of our common life as well, "how we treat our spouse and children, the way we drive our cars, and the media we take in."[23]

Ask God to help you identify areas of your life which you have not surrendered and opened to the working of the Holy Spirit. Ask the Holy Spirit to help you have a deeper desire to surrender your life totally. You may want to find a prayer partner who will join with you in this prayer and hold you accountable for it.

6

Transformation: Participation in the Work of the Holy Spirit

I also have the responsibility to keep my spirit in agreement with His Spirit. And when I do, Jesus gradually lifts me up to the level where He lived—a level of perfect submission to His Father's will—where I pay no attention to anything else.

—OSWALD CHAMBERS

We have observed that being created in the image of God means that we are relational as the Persons of the Holy Trinity are relational; we are designed in a way that our fullness of life is found in relationship with God. That relationship was broken by sin, but sin is more than something we have done, it is who we are without God's work in us. Thus, spiritual formation is more than mastering a list of activities. It is a transformation to something, to holiness. Only the Holy Spirit touches us at the depth at which this change needs to be made.

It is important to emphasize again that sanctification occurs at the initiative of God and God alone. As justification—that initial conversion of the believer—is a work of grace, so sanctification—the process of becoming like Jesus—also is a work of grace. However, unlike justification, in sanctification the grace of God allows for and even requires the participation of the believer. Recognizing God's promise of escape from the depravity caused by evil desires and instead sharing in his divine nature, Peter called believers to "make every effort to respond to God's promises" (2 Peter 1:5). Paul reminded the believers at Philippi, "Work hard to show the results of your salvation, obeying God with deep reverence and fear" (Phil. 2:12). Paul further pointed to the synergy between grace and works in sanctification when he said, "That's why I work and struggle so hard, depending on Christ's mighty power that works within me" (Col. 1:29). At one and the same time, Paul worked to be like Christ and depended on the power of Christ to change him. Just in this manner, believers participate in God's gracious work of sanctification.

The result is "that anyone who belongs to Christ has become a new person. The old life is gone; a new life has begun!" (2 Cor. 5:17). The believer's transformation begins and is continually assisted by the grace of God. However, action or participation by the believer is indispensable. I had a friend in college who was a philosophy major. While visiting his home one day, his father asked him what he was going to do with his degree. My friend told me that he pointed to a hammock in the back-yard and told his dad he was going to stretch out in the hammock, get comfortable, and think. I don't know how that dream of a passive life worked out for him. Coming from a farming community, I suspect the next time he went home the hammock had been replaced with a shovel and a hoe. Our sanctification is a work of the Holy Spirit, but it means anything but a passive life for us. Chambers described this relationship: "I also have the responsibility to keep my spirit in agreement with His Spirit. And when I do, Jesus gradually lifts me up to the level where He lived—a level of perfect submission to His Father's will—where I pay no attention to anything else."[1]

God, in his sovereignty, has ordained that this process will not be completed absent certain actions of the believer. Still, the grace of sanctification is a gift, not something that can be earned by even the hardest of work.

This gracious act of God and the believer's response are inseparable from the regeneration that occurs in the new birth. Augustine allowed for some degree of collaboration by the believer in the work of the Holy Spirit in one's spiritual life. Wesley's view of regeneration was that "believers are empowered by the presence of the Holy Spirit in their hearts to engage in divine/human cooperation."[2] This joint endeavor does not imply that the role of God and the role of the believer are equal or equally difficult. God's role is prior, primary, and beyond our ability to achieve. Nevertheless, there are two roles.

Because it is a change in nature motivated by the Holy Spirit, the manner in which transformation occurs will always have an element of mystery. Indeed it is a mysterious union with the death and resurrection of Jesus in which the domination of the flesh is defeated. Paul's admonitions concerning the mind of Christ (1 Corinthians 2:16; Philippians 2:5) suggest that a person changes from being driven by self-referenced desires to one who has the perspective of Christ's own Spirit. While this transformation might not be understood precisely, we do have some insight into how the process occurs. Wesley understood part of the event to be epistemological, an awakening of previously dormant spiritual senses and an understanding of a new way of living. It involves the beginning of the understanding of a new nature and identity given as a gift from God. The believer begins to comprehend that she was created in the image of God, as one designed to live in unity with God, as a beloved child of the Father. With a corrected understanding of one's identity, value, meaning, and purpose come new desires and new motivations. The scriptural mandate to "let the Holy Spirit guide your lives" (Gal. 5:16) points to a life in which we are constantly measuring our thoughts, feelings, and acts "against biblical principles illuminated by the Holy Spirit, and drawing upon his power to order and direct these according to the will of God."[3] The essential skill that God develops in us is to know how to measure thinking and behavior against Scripture.

Dallas Willard described the process of spiritual transformation in terms of the ordering of the six basic aspects of human nature—thought, feeling, choice, body, social context, and soul. He wrote, "The ideal of the spiritual life in the Christian understanding is one where all of the essential parts of the human self are effectively organized around God, as they are restored and sustained by him."[4] In addition, he wrote:

> I constantly and thoughtfully engage myself with the ideas, images, and information that are provided by God through the Scriptures, his Son

Jesus, and the lives and experiences of his people through the ages. In doing that, I am constantly nourished by the Holy Spirit in ways far beyond my own efforts or understanding. What I receive in response to my efforts is therefore also a gift, a grace. Spiritual (trans)formation of my thought life is achieved by the ministry of the Spirit in the midst of my necessary and well-directed efforts.[5]

We find that all Persons of the Trinity work in our spiritual formation, it being initiated as a work of grace by the Father. It begins with justification through the life, death, and resurrection of Jesus. Justification is accompanied by regeneration through the Holy Spirit, who gives the believer a new status and freedom from the bondage of sin. God the Father "continues to provide grace, the Son Jesus serves as the believer's role model, and the Holy Spirit works inside the believer's heart to continue to enlighten, illuminate, and empower his heart to obey God's will and grow into holiness."[6] We believers are no longer condemned by sin but rather can live in the eternal truth of victory through Jesus. Paul told us that since we have new life in Christ, we are to set our sights on the realities of heaven (Colossians 3:1). Live today in the certainty of the promises that remain forever true. When we can live for eternity rather than for the immediate gratification of temporary desires, we will live according to a new understanding of who we truly are.

A verse that expresses well the work of the Holy Spirit and the participation of the believer is 1 John 1:9: "But if we confess our sins to him, he is faithful and just to forgive us our sins and to cleanse us from all wickedness."

The action to which we are called (confession, or repentance) and the resulting infusion of grace are both seen in this verse in the forgiveness of sin and the cleansing of the believer. The believer confesses and God responds in grace.

This work to which we are called, true repentance, emerges directly from the point of our deepest need, the place where God encounters the sinful nature. In King David's repentance for his sin with Bathsheba, he asked for much, much more than release from accountability for his sin. He asked for cleansing, that God would create in him a clean heart (Psalm 51:10). In other words, he asked that God would *put a new nature in him.* This is true repentance and it is more than an admission of guilt, an apology, or a promise to stop. The New Testament also instructs on repentance:

> In the New Testament, repentance (*metanoia*) is used to describe the changing of one's mind. In true repentance, then, the seeker changes his mind not only about God but also about himself and his sin. This involves not only a turning away from sin, but also a turning toward God with humility and conviction.[7]

True repentance invites and seeks transformation. If sin is properly termed a heart curved in on itself, repentance is a turning toward God, which turns the most basic direction of a person's life from being curved inward upon self to being refocused upon God and others. The Holy Spirit works in the life of the believer, convicting of sin while illuminating an alternative to a life opposed to God, and the awakened believer responds in repentance. Grace changes our loyalties from ourselves and the things of the world to God and the things of heaven (Colossians 3:2).

Looking again at 1 John 1:9, the need for both forgiveness and cleansing are expressed—forgiveness of sin and a cleansing that brings a refocusing of the believer's nature upon God. The "sin that goes before a sin," of which Augustine wrote, means "the distorted will 'to live according to man rather than according to God.'"[8]

Or, as many have said, "We are not sinners because we sin; we sin because we are sinners." The heart or mind of the person is already polluted with something that is opposed to the authority of God or the idea of surrender—something that sets itself up against the life of purity and discipline.[9]

This opposition to God is the substance of the fallen nature and, therefore, must be the object of our true repentance. Participation in the work of the Holy Spirit calls for confession of both our sin and our sin nature, which requires a self-awareness that brings both into the light. It seeks not only forgiveness for breaking the rule but also correction of the self-centered passion lying underneath.

The disciple of Jesus participates in the work of the Holy Spirit through many spiritual disciplines that are sometimes called the *means of grace*. This latter phrase has long been used in the church to represent the manner in which believers dispose themselves toward God's gift of grace. Spiritual disciplines are means through which the grace of God is naturally received. It is really as simple as this. We are promised that when we pray the grace of God will come through his answer. Prayer is a means through which God shows his grace. When we read the Bible we are promised that the Holy Spirit will use that discipline to teach us, to lead us into truth. Reading the Bible is a means through which God shows his grace. Thomas Merton gave an analogy from plant life. As a plant grows, blooms, and bears specific fruit by its intrinsic nature, so a disciple of Jesus will be formed into the likeness of Christ by engaging with a proper heart in the means of grace.[10]

The means of grace are not an invitation to work harder. The means of grace are not meritorious in themselves. They do not earn brownie points, God's favor, or God's blessing. They are simply a means of opening oneself to the "empowering grace of God in our regular daily walk with God, as we rest in Christ. They are ways of putting up our sails so to speak, to catch the wind of God's Spirit driving us along toward Christlikeness."[11]

Jesus' life certainly exemplified attention to the disciplines including prayer, fasting, reliance on the Word of God, and solitude. Paul followed Jesus by living as Jesus lived. Wesley understood living as Jesus lived to be a focused, uninterrupted way of life: "If Wesley could say anything about the spiritual life to contemporary Christians, it might well be, 'God does not call you to have a devotional time; God calls you to live a devotional life.'"[12] In other words, our nature should be such that we live within these means of grace. Instructing his converts, Wesley divided the means of grace into two categories that would have been familiar in his Anglican Church—instituted and prudential. The instituted means of grace, or works of devotion, include prayer, study of the Word, the Lord's Supper, fasting, and the corporate life of believers.

Prudential means of grace, or works of mercy, include doing no harm, doing good, and attending the ordinances of God. To this list could be added a number of different practices, including solitude, silence, chastity, confession, and submission.

The growth that we seek and receive from engaging in the means of grace comes not from the activities themselves, but the empowerment of the Holy Spirit. This obedience leads to Christlikeness and deeper intimacy with God. We cannot measure our spiritual maturity by the number of disciplines in which we engage, such as how much we pray, how much we read the Word, or how much we give. The blessing in the means of grace is not in ritual or habit:

> At first glance, we tend to think of spiritual formation as learning biblical principles. In reality, an intellectual knowledge about God is not the same as trusting in God's sufficiency in the midst of our fears and needs. Spiritual formation takes place only when we struggle with the dark aspects of our lives and experience God's work of transformation. It must extend to our hearts, not just our heads.[13]

The efficacy of the means of grace lies in their ability to open the believer to the transforming power of the Holy Spirit. In his sermon "Causes of the Inefficacy of Christianity," Wesley asked why in its long history Christianity seems to have had so little impact, even in those locations in which it is a well-established part of society. He referred to a saying common among Christians of the early church, "The soul and the body make a man;

the spirit and discipline make a Christian," and arrived at the conclusion that this inefficacy grows out of the failure to add Christian discipline to Christian doctrine. Spiritual disciplines, or means of grace, are exercises in turning away from self-sufficiency, away from the fallen self, and turning the heart in trust toward God.

Life lived in this pattern results in inward change that manifests in righteous outward actions. The goal is change in the very nature of the believer, something that will bear fruit in outward behavior. It is quite simply called a change of heart because the Bible teaches that actions are determined by the condition of the heart (Matthew 12:34; Luke 6:45). This concept of inward change may be observed in the teaching of Jesus when, for instance, he focused attention not only on the outward act of murder but also on the inward thoughts of anger (Matthew 5:21–26) or not only the act of adultery but also the inward lusts from which adultery proceeds (Matthew 5:27–30). As put by Keith Meyer:

> We can dive into programs that incorporate spiritual practices into our lives, yet if these practices don't result in life change—if there is no solid instruction on how to actually change habits of anger, rage, lust, contempt, and control—we may simply redouble our religious activity. Without a vision for a new kind of life and the means to appropriate that life, our best intentions will just produce more of what we already have.[14]

This is extremely important because hypocrisy and legalism can be the results of religion that focuses only on external behavior.

The spiritual disciplines are means used by God to bestow his grace upon people. The promise to the believer is that as he or she engages in these disciplines God will be faithful to respond in grace. Certainly his response will be in his way and according to what he knows is good, but the believer proceeds with trust in the promise. Grace is God's action in the lives of believers that helps them accomplish something they could not on their own. In some God-ordained way, grace awakens the redeemed, regenerated spirit, causing it to unfold toward its Creator as a bloom unfolds toward the sun. Thomas Merton wrote, "It calls us to reach out for a more abundant life, a fuller knowledge of God, a deeper sounding of the depths of our own selves and a more perfect and more generous giving of ourselves to the love and service of other men."[15]

Paul explained the working of these spiritual exercises using the example of an athlete who through discipline prepares for successful competition (1 Corinthians 9:25). Like the athlete, we prepare through the means of grace to compete successfully against those powers that draw us away from Jesus (Philippians 3:14). Considering again just one of these in brief example, reading Scripture works as a means of grace. Scripture has always been the primary source of knowing God and his plan for the world, for us, and for eternity. Reading Scripture may be a means for the grace of God if that reading is guided by the Holy Spirit. Through such reading of Scripture, we begin to see the world through the eyes of Jesus and even feel it through his heart. As the truth in Scripture is embraced, it tears out what is old and corrupt and refurbishes life with what is new, holy, and alive in Christ Jesus. "[Kenneth] Boa suggests that renewing our mind by internalizing biblical values through a daily program of 'reading, memorizing, meditating on and personalizing Scripture' is the antidote to the worldly enticement."[16] The things of this world grow strangely dim as the things of God grow brighter and more real. Chambers wrote:

> Perseverance means more than endurance—more than simply holding on until the end. A saint's life is in the hands of God like a bow and arrow in the hands of an archer. God is aiming at something the saint cannot see, but our Lord continues to stretch and strain, and every once in a while the saint says, "I can't take any more." Yet God pays no attention; He goes on stretching until His purpose is in sight, and then He lets the arrow fly. Entrust yourself to God's hands.[17]

The practice of the means of grace has been the subject of scholarly writing since the very beginning of the exploration of the relationship between God and his creation. The writings are voluminous and cover well each of the disciplines. That being the case, I make no effort in this book to address the practice of specific disciplines or the benefits of such practice. The point is that unless the believer engages in these spiritual disciplines, promised grace will be forfeited. Dallas Willard argued that "the misunderstanding of the spiritual disciplines' place in life has been responsible for Protestantism's adopting 'cheap grace' as the dominant mode of its recent existence."[18] God loves to bless his children and the grace that comes through the practice of the spiritual disciplines is one of his great blessings.

Finally, anticipating a temptation to reject participation in the work of the Holy Spirit on the basis of the Reformation's rejection of salvation by works, remember that this work is for sanctification, not justification. "Effort in the spiritual life is good. The Scriptures extol its benefits (see 1 Corinthians 9:24–27; Galatians 6:7–9; Colossians 1:28–29; 1 Timothy 4:7; Hebrews 5:14)."[19] Grace does not make room for earning, but it does allow for effort.[20]

This gracious action of the Holy Spirit working with and through our efforts has often been illustrated through the image of the sailor and the wind. The wind is present without any contribution or effort from the sailor. He cannot cause the wind or determine the direction from which it blows. He cannot influence the strength of the wind. What the sailor *can* do is unfurl the sail and turn it in a direction to best catch the wind. Thus, the wind and the sailor work together to move the boat along toward its destination. In our spiritual formation, such participation is graciously allowed and used by the indwelling Holy Spirit.

Reflection and Application

1. How might you visualize or express this idea of participating in the work of the Holy Spirit in your spiritual formation? What hope do you find from this biblical truth?

2. Consider reflectively the following quote from Dallas Willard:

   > I constantly and thoughtfully engage myself with the ideas, images, and information that are provided by God through the Scriptures, his Son Jesus, and the lives and experiences of his people through the ages. In doing that, I am constantly nourished by the Holy Spirit in ways far beyond my own efforts or understanding. What I receive in response to my efforts is therefore also a gift, a grace. Spiritual (trans)formation of my thought life is achieved by the ministry of the Spirit in the midst of my necessary and well-directed efforts.[21]

   What guidance for your spiritual formation and your leading others in their spiritual formation do you get from this quote?

3. Dennis Kinlaw wrote:

   > From Paul's admonitions concerning the mind of Christ (1 Corinthians 2:16; Philippians 2:5), it may be concluded that a person changes from

being driven by physical desires to one who has "the perspective of Christ's own Spirit."[22]

These physical desires could include the desire for power, intimacy, security, respect, and comfort.

- What does it mean to have "the perspective of Christ's own Spirit"? How does this contrast with the perspective of the fallen self? Push yourself past the superficial level in answering this.
- What understanding and motivation might come from the work of the Holy Spirit in this transformation?
- How is trust in God a part of this transformation?

4. Reflect on the statement made that the means of grace are not an invitation to work harder. The means of grace are not meritorious in themselves. They do not earn God's favor, or God's blessing. How would you say this in your own words in order to give guidance to someone seeking your counsel to develop their spiritual disciplines?

5. How is practice of the means of grace a discipline of turning from self-sufficiency to reliance on or trust in God's sufficiency?

7

The Assurance of
the Love of God

*Nothing is so fundamental to the Christian journey as
knowing and feeling that we are loved. Nothing. This is
the basis for the whole of what it means to be a Christian.*

—GORDON T. SMITH

Paul wrote in Romans 5 that in human experience, self-sacrifice is unusual even when the one for whom the sacrifice is made is especially good (Romans 5:8). He drew a contrast with God's love—sacrificial love that defines the very nature of God—love that is not determined by the qualities of the one loved. Rather, from a nature that defies human logic and wisdom, God loved us even while we were still sinners and hence enemies of God's sovereign plan for creation (Romans 5:7). This love is known in a multitude of ways and is confirmed by the gift of the Holy Spirit who fills the believer's heart with the love of God (Romans 5:5). The ultimate confirmation of God's love came through the horrific sacrifice of Jesus on the cross. Through many acts, the Creator God reaches out to his creation, forming a basis for a profound inner assurance of the love of God. John R. W. Stott wrote:

> The unique majesty of God's love lies in the combination of three factors, namely that when Christ died for us, God (a) was giving himself, (b) even to the horrors of a sin-bearing death on the cross, and (c) doing so for his undeserving enemies.[1]

This love of God is the environment in which the follower of Jesus lives and breathes. It follows, then, that spiritual formation *must* be pursued within this context and an accepting and grateful awareness of the grand reality that accompanies an assurance of the love of God.

Many have written to remind the student of spiritual formation that this quest for supreme human fulfillment is not about winning or earning the love of God. However, if the assurance of the love of God is not securely established as the setting in which spiritual formation is pursued, then the heart of the journey will almost certainly become distorted and misguided. Spiritual formation is a demanding, lifelong journey that can lead to discouragement if our heart is not sustained and encouraged by the assurance of God's unfathomable love acting as a safety net. But with this assurance—this promise of victory already won firmly in place—spiritual formation becomes an addition to something already wonderful, our eternal life with God.

Chambers wrote, "My assurance is to be built upon God's assurance to me. God says, 'I will never leave you,' so that then I may boldly say, 'The Lord is my helper; I will not fear.'"[2] The assurance of God's love is an underlying necessity in the life and spiritual formation of a disciple of Jesus:

> Nothing is so fundamental to the Christian journey as knowing and feeling that we are loved. Nothing. This is the basis for the whole of what it means to be a Christian. There is no other foundation on which we can build. It is from the experience of God's love that we know the grace of God and live out every other dimension of our Christian faith.[3]

By God's grace through persevering faith in Jesus, our status as a child of God is secure. Spiritual formation engaged with our focus fixed on the love of God helps us realize the present marvelous reality that is offered to us:

> Imagine our amazement, our utter shock, when we finally understood that Jesus actually loves us and never leaves us! That our sin does not stand between Jesus and us. That Jesus, who is the centerpiece of this realm of grace, actually walks around our sin, stands with His arm around us, with our sin in front of us, and gives us His perspective on our sin. He never leaves. Well, that changes everything![4]

The histories of spiritual formation are filled with those who struggled and failed and felt brutalized by their failure. Early in his ministry, Wesley sought to record in his diary his spiritual life in minute detail, recording each resolution kept or broken, the level of his commitment to devotion, and other activities associated with his effort to spend every minute of his life in the service of God. This proved to be a terribly defeating method of discipline. It was not until Wesley's Aldersgate experience that he came to feel his heart "strangely warmed," an experience that brought his devotion within the sphere of the assurance of God's love. Prior to that, Wesley described himself as one who "fell and rose and fell again." After Aldersgate, while Wesley continued to develop in his understanding of the full meaning of salvation through faith, his struggles were more and more *within* the assurance of the love of God, the assurance that affords the believer the basis upon which to pursue Christlikeness with unfailing confidence and hope.

The nature of God's love means that nothing can be done to make God love a person more. Let's personalize that. There is absolutely nothing you can do to make God love you more. He loved people (you) fully even when they were his enemies. Now by his grace he loves you as his friend. "We cannot earn this love, manipulate things to make God love us more or in any way make ourselves more loveable. Nothing can make this love increase; we are already loved to the full."[5] God does not love us for who we are, for what we do, or for what we accomplish. *We are, quite simply, loved.*

This is so contrary to our human nature that it's hard to accept. It goes against the earning-favor pattern that we know in human relationships. It goes against the performance-based acceptance that is so deeply embedded in our culture. But it is an extremely important truth. Thomas à Kempis added breadth to this description of love when he reminded us that God loves us as much in our failings as he does in our successes. Try to get your head around that! That's not a rhetorical suggestion. Really, try! Does that take some pressure off? This is a truth of invaluable worth, yet one that is so hard for us to apply in the day-to-day routine of life. But to the extent life is lived with this assurance, it is a freeing truth that allows a follower of Jesus to know the joy and peace of God.

The assurance offered by the awareness of God's love is not to be projected forward to a distant time and place but rather is to be known and experienced here and now. It's not that God will love us someday when we get to heaven. His love for us is a present reality. When this assurance is properly embraced by the disciple of Jesus, it affords the greatest opportunity to grow into a healthy view of self. Looking again at the Genesis account of the fall in light of the subsequent history of humankind leads to the clear conclusion that the fall was *the tragic event* of all history. As the heart turned inward upon itself, the fallen self took God's rightful place on the throne, and people have struggled with this disoriented self ever since. So, we can see how self-denial has come to be understood as central to the process of sanctification. An often-cited biblical basis for the centrality of self-denial is Jesus' admonition to his disciples, "If any of you wants to be my follower, you must turn from your selfish ways, take up your cross, and follow me" (Matt. 16:24). While Jesus does indeed call for self-denial, we need a proper understanding of the denial of self if room is to be left for a healthy view of self.

Self-denial is understood as a spiritual or physical denial of self that seeks separation from undesirable influences of the world. In self-denial we reject some improper gratification of a desire. Self-denial pursued from an improper understanding or poor sense of self-worth can actually hinder one's spiritual formation. Such a misunderstanding can lead believers to think of themselves as vile and worthless, and can manifest itself in various harmful, destructive ways such as self-flagellation or crawling for miles on bloody knees in an effort to merit forgiveness and win God's approval. There are other, more subtle manifestations such as fasting to the point of detriment to one's health. A distorted view of self and its denial is not only potentially harmful, it also lacks a sound biblical basis.

The denial that produces proper spiritual formation is the denial of the *fallen* self, not the self in totality.[6] It is the denial of that aspect of the self that seeks satisfaction through improper means. Danger lurks when one's view of self becomes negative to an excessive degree. From his ascetic life in North Africa, Charles de Foucauld learned the danger of focusing too much on oneself and one's own unworthiness rather than on Jesus. A proper focus, he wrote, keeps in view "that love which made him endure such sufferings for each one of us, and which makes it so sweet and pleasant and natural to him to give us the greatest blessings."[7] The writer of the book of Hebrews said of Jesus, "Because of the joy awaiting him, he endured the cross, disregarding its shame" (Heb. 12:2). *You are the joy awaiting him!* This balanced view sees in the horror of the crucifixion the awful potential of the fallen self, but it also sees in the heart of Jesus love for the Father and for all of humanity that both motivated and sustained him in that heartbreaking time.

The doctrine of total depravity is somewhat heavy theology but as a widely held view on the nature of humankind it holds an important position in any discussion of the value of human beings. It addresses the inability of human beings to choose to follow God, refrain from evil, or accept the gift of salvation without the prevenient grace of God. A casual consideration of the doctrine could at first blush seem to leave nothing of worth in the self. It is a doctrine that deserves careful application. David K. Clark wrote, "Traditionally, *total* has referred to the extent of the depravity, not its degree. It is not that the aspects of human personality are 100% corrupted (degree). Rather, 100% of them (extent) are depraved."[8] The doctrine acknowledges the total lostness of the fallen nature while leaving room for a healthy view of the self, including a carefully and humbly developed self-respect. Without diminishing our entire dependence on God, an abundant Christian life needs a positive attitude toward self, that is, the self created by God in His image. Henri Nouwen observed, "Over the years I have come to realize that the greatest trap in our life is not success, popularity, or power, but self-rejection."[9] An embrace of the assurance of God's love that promotes a healthy view of self resists destructive and demeaning attitudes of self-rejection.

Clear understanding and unambiguous terminology are essential. The biblical picture of human nature is neither simply optimistic nor pessimistic. The Bible does teach that men and women are unworthy of God and unable to change that fact through self-effort, but it also talks about the worth of humanity in the eyes of God. Deeper reflection reveals a deeper truth. "We are not worthy of God's salvation, but we are worthful, full of worth. We may not deserve to be saved, but we are worth saving. We cannot earn salvation, but we are of value to God."[10] This distinction between worthy and worthful is of great importance. We should never regard our worthfulness as merited, achieved, or earned. It is given to us as a gift.

This worth or value of which Clark wrote finds its basis in the fact that humanity was created in the image of God. God designed into each of us a nature that is worthful. I heard a story about a couple that bought a sweater at a second-hand clothing store for 58 cents. The sweater had the words West Point across the front. They later noticed the name Lombardi written on a patch of cloth sown on the inside but didn't think much of it until they watched a documentary on the life of the legendary coach Vince Lombardi. Lombardi had coached at Army early in his career. After being verified as a sweater once owned by the famous coach, the sweater was put up for auction and it sold for more than $42,000. There was nothing about the old sweater itself that gave it such value. Its value came from the coach who at one time had owned it.

Jesus spoke of humankind as having value, but even more so he acted as if humankind had value. He put on humanity in the incarnation. John 3:16 provides assurance that God's love for the world is so great that he gave his only Son that all might have the offer of eternal life. Individualized, this verse says that God's love for me, a sinner, is so great that he gave his Son for my redemption. I have to ask myself, *Do I really let this truth sink in so deeply that it affects everything I do and everything I am?* This giving of such great magnitude reflects astounding value in the one for whom the gift is given. But, the value should not be understood as originating in the one saved so his or her life somehow equates with the life of Jesus, value for value. Rather, the value comes from the giver and the giving. The value comes from God and what he has done. The result is that I, the one for whom the gift is given, can know with assurance that I am a beloved of God. I don't know fully what that means, and I suspect I will be learning more about God's love throughout eternity, but I know enough to be certain that it changes everything.

A healthy view of oneself is necessary for sustained growth in Christlikeness. This important understanding has not always come easily in Christian tradition, challenged as it is with the human fondness to work things out independently and the convenient remedy of self-denial. Since God judges the heart, the heart or attitude in self-denial becomes of paramount importance:

> Proper self-sacrifice is not self-sacrifice for its own sake, but rather needs to be oriented towards the good. . . . The Christian tradition has perhaps tended to warn more forcefully of the dangers of improper self-love than of improper self-sacrifice. But either, taken to an extreme, can be both practically disastrous and incompatible with the Christian ideal.[11]

When dealing with self-denial and self-worth, care must be taken to avoid self-referenced attitudes in whatever form or shape they may be found. Christlikeness is to be sought in order to be all Jesus saved the believer to be (Philippians 3:12). Being all Jesus saved us to be cannot be directed solely toward ourselves. It necessarily includes

Christlikeness for the sake of others. We can see this in the pattern of Abraham. Abraham was without doubt personally blessed by the promises of God. However, as God made clear, Abraham was blessed not just for himself but that he might be a blessing to others, even all nations (Genesis 12:2). Likewise, the fullness of this blessing may be seen in the greatest of the commandments, which includes both love of God and love of neighbor (Matthew 22:38–39). Therein lies one of the keys to spiritual formation, blessed to be a blessing, or being available to God for the sake of others. Spiritual formation led by the Holy Spirit will always embrace a reference to the Other and the other.

This brings us back to the pursuit of spiritual formation within the assurance of the love of God firmly in place. Attitude in self-denial will make all the difference. Whether one's self-denial is positively humble or negatively demeaning may depend on how the believer sees himself or herself in the love of Jesus, which love is a divine act of grace. A marvelous promise is found in the baptism of Jesus. When Jesus came up out of the water after his baptism, a voice from heaven said, "This is my dearly beloved Son, who brings me great joy" (Matt. 3:17). Note that at this point Jesus had performed no miracles nor had his obedience led him to the cross.

Consider some other words of the Father to the Son. One of many prophecies fulfilled by Jesus was the prophecy of Isaiah, "Look at my Servant, whom I have chosen. He is my Beloved, who pleases me" (Matt. 12:18). During the transfiguration of Jesus, the affirming voice of the Father is heard saying, "This is my Son, my Chosen One"

(Luke 9:35). Likewise, throughout the New Testament there are many references to believers as those who have been chosen by God. As the believer is majestically and mysteriously brought within the inter-relationships of the Trinity, there comes the extravagant opportunity to each and every one of us to understand we have been personally and individually chosen as a beloved by God. In his High Priestly Prayer, Jesus affirmed the extent of the love the Father has for each of us as a disciple of Jesus. The extent of this love is measured against nothing less than the love of the Father for Jesus.

The unfathomable revelation Jesus conveyed in this prayer is that this love is the same; the Father loves you, a disciple of Jesus, as much as he loves Jesus himself (John 17:11–23). As children of God, believers are God's chosen ones. Henri Nouwen wrote,

> You must hold on to the truth that you are the chosen one. That truth is the bedrock on which you can build a life as the Beloved. When you lose touch with your chosenness, you expose yourself to the temptation of self-rejection, and that temptation undermines the possibility of ever growing as the Beloved.[12]

In *The Return of the Prodigal Son*, Nouwen explored the love of God through the homecoming in this parable (Luke 15:11–32). The parable helps us understand that home is where God is and abiding there is our greatest spiritual challenge. We tend to leave home, ignoring the place of true love and instead looking for love elsewhere. But it is in this true home that we can hear God say to us, "You are my beloved, on you my favor rests." We so easily become deaf to that voice, instead being overcome by voices that say we are a mistake, a burden, stupid, and worthless. These voices try to call us to the impossible task of proving our worth through intelligence, wealth, or what we do. This was the voice in the wilderness that tried to deceive Jesus into thinking he had to prove himself by being successful, popular, and powerful. But Jesus understood it is not this world that defines us.[13]

Recognition and acceptance of the depth of the love of God is a personal transformation. Most can remember the agony and the joy of the childhood playground when teams were being chosen, players being selected one by one. What about me? Will I be chosen? Joy and relief when your name was called. You had been chosen! How incomparably and wonderfully complete and eternal is the knowledge that God has chosen you. You need no longer fear not being chosen. Your name has been called! This is the assurance of God's love. This is the value of the self. This is the foundation upon which we understand that we are the beloved of God.

Nouwen wrote that our ability to enjoy the good things of the world hinges on the ability we have to receive them as affirmations of the truth that we are the beloved of God. We are accepted! We must learn to accept and live in the truth of that acceptance. This loving acceptance can be seen every day in many places but nowhere greater than in the cross. "The unfathomable depths of our belovedness is revealed in the cruciform love of God in Christ."[14]

The call to holiness that draws the believer in spiritual formation must never be separated from the assurance of the love of God. The believer must remain anchored in both the holiness of God and the love of God—holy love. Self-denial properly guided by the eternal love of God can lead to the discovery of the true self, a self that discovers who it was created to be in and through the love of God. Without such a balance, voices that call us worthless and unlovable—whether coming from the outside or from within—are more likely to lead to self-rejection, which spirals down into either arrogance or in low self-esteem. A healthy view of self does not begin with self-rejection but rather is guided by God's acceptance and commitment to his beloved. It is a God-referenced source of value and meaning that allows a believer to have an appropriate and healthy view of self.

Reflection and Application

1. Look for and describe the assurance of God's love that you hear in the following passage:

   > Jesus says, "Are you tired? Worn out? Burned out on religion? Come to me. Get away with me and you'll recover your life. I'll show you how to take a real rest. Walk with me and work with me—watch how I do it. Learn the unforced rhythms of grace. I won't lay anything heavy or ill-fitting on you. Keep company with me and you'll learn to live freely and lightly. (Matt. 11:28–30 THE MESSAGE)

2. How would you describe to someone the difference between proper self-denial and improper, destructive self-denial?

3. In your own words, why is it important to engage in spiritual formation with the assurance of the love of God? How might your spiritual formation be different if approached with a deeper acceptance of this assurance?

4. Compose and write out a prayer about the assurance of the love of God. This prayer may address thankfulness for what you understand, petition for greater under- standing, help in applying the assurance of the love of God in your life, and wisdom in sharing this revealed truth of the love of God with others. You may want to share this with someone to whom you are accountable with the prayer request that the assurance of God's love penetrate more and more deeply into your life as a disciple of Jesus.

Epilogue

God set before Adam and Eve life and death. Adam and Eve entered the garden of Eden as part of God's perfect creation but left through disobedience into death. When given the opportunity to demonstrate their trust in God, they chose to trust their own way. The trust that was expected of them was the simplest of trust. It required no overt action on their part. They needed only to refrain from doing something, eating from the tree of the knowledge of good and evil. Exercise of this trust would not cause pain or humiliation, nor was their well-being threatened in any way by not eating. The failure in this simple expectation of trust was of such significance that Adam and Eve received the penalty of death and were stripped of intimacy with God.

Generations later, as the Israelites traveled from bondage in Egypt to the Promised Land, God set before them the same choice. "Today I have given you the choice between life and death, between blessings and curses. . . . Oh, that you would choose life, so that you and your descendants might live!" (Deut. 30:19). Life was to be chosen by loving God, obeying and committing to him. The history of Israel is one in which they consistently chose their own way instead of God's way.

In the early days of the church, Paul wrote about life or death in terms of the power of the law and the power of sin (Romans 7:4–12). The power of the law lies in its condemnation of those who fail to keep its just requirements. Jesus has removed the power of the law, its ability to condemn, and the penalty of death for all who accept him as Savior. He did this by his obedience even to death on the cross.

But the power of sin remains and hence so does a choice between life and death. The power of sin lies in its ability to entice people into disobedience and to deceive them into believing true life can be found through sin. As enticing as it may seem, this is the way of death. "There is a path before each person that seems right, but it ends in death" (Prov. 14:12). The answer Jesus provides is that he is the way, the truth, and the life, and that he came that those who come to him might have a "rich and satisfying life" (John 10:10), or "fullness of life" in some translations.

In the garden of Gethsemane, Jesus was called to trust in the Father even though it meant betrayal, humiliation, the pain of a horrible crucifixion, and death. It was a place at which trust required Jesus to surrender everything to the Father. The trust Jesus placed in the Father led through the cross to resurrection, ascension to the right hand of God, and true life for all who believe in this marvelous salvation that comes by the grace of God. Freedom from the power of sin comes as the promised indwelling Holy Spirit convicts, urges, and empowers the believer, allowing him or her to see in Jesus true life as God intended and to be transformed into such a life.

Today, God sets before his beloved children life or death, true life or false life. Seeking to find true life through the false enticements of Satan and the world around us is to live as a slave to sin. It is the false life, the way of death. Because the just requirements of the law have been satisfied by Jesus, the believer is free to live a life of no condemnation—free to find true life in Christlikeness, holiness, the image of God. The law is a guide to a life in which the believer seeks to love God with all his heart, soul, mind, and strength, and to love his neighbor as one just as important to God, a neighbor also created in the image of God.

Notes

Introduction

1. "The Fool's Prayer," Edward Rowland Sill, 1841–1887.

Chapter 1: The Image of God

1. Saint Augustine, *Confessions*, trans. R. S. Pine-Coffin (London: Penguin Books, 1961), 21.

2. Anders Lund Jacobsen, "Genesis 1–3 as Source for the Anthropology of Origen," *Vigiliae Christianae* 62.3 (2008): 218.

3. Mel Lawrenz, *The Dynamics of Spiritual Formation* (Grand Rapids, MI: Baker Books, 2000), 145–46.

4. W. S. Towner, "Clones of God," *Interpretation: A Journal of Bible & Theology* 59.4 (2005): 341–42.

5. Luder G. Whitlock, "Spiritual Direction in the Reformed Tradition," *Journal of Psychology and Theology* (Winter 2002): 319.

6. The idea of theōsis, so central in the theology of the Eastern Church, has appeared problematic to the West with its commitment to the otherness of God. However, this conflict "becomes less worrisome if we think of spirituality not as becoming part of a divine 'substance' but as entering into the dynamic life of the trinitarian God" (F. Leron Shults and Steven J. Sandage, *Transforming Spirituality: Integrating Theology and Psychology* [Grand Rapids: Baker Academic, 2006], 53.)

7. Towner, "Clones of God," 342.

8. Paul Sands, "The Imago Dei as Vocation," *Evangelical Quarterly* 82.1 (2010): 38.

9. M. Robert Mulholland Jr., *The Deeper Journey: The Spirituality of Discovering Your True Self* (Downers Grove, IL: InterVarsity, 2006), 16.

10. Ibid., 38–39.

11. T. A. Smail, "In the Image of the Triune God," *International Journal of Systematic Theology* 5.1 (2003): 23; see Colossians 3:10.

12. Ibid.

13. M. Robert Mulholland Jr., "Revelation," *Cornerstone Biblical Commentary*, ed. Philip W. Comfort (Carol Stream, IL: Tyndale, 2011), 481.

14. Steve DeNeff, *7 Saving Graces: Living Above the Deadly Sins* (Indianapolis, IN: Wesleyan, 2010), 32–33.

15. Smail, "In the Image of the Triune God," 23.

16. M. Robert Mulholland Jr., *Shaped by the Word: The Power of Scripture in Spiritual Formation* (Nashville, TN: The Upper Room, 1985), 26.

17. Oswald Chambers, *My Utmost for His Highest: An Updated Edition in Today's English*, ed. James Reimann (Grand Rapids, MI: Discovery House, 1992), March 13.

Chapter 2: The Fall

1. Thomas Merton, *The New Man* (New York: Farrar, 1962), 53.

2. Dennis F. Kinlaw, *Let's Start with Jesus: A New Way of Doing Theology* (Grand Rapids, MI: Zondervan, 2005), 108.

3. A. W. Tozer, *The Pursuit of God* (Camp Hill, PA: Christian Publications, 1982), 60.

4. David G. Benner, *The Gift of Being Yourself: The Sacred Call to Self-Discovery* (Downers Grove, IL: InterVarsity Press, 2004), 42.

5. Dallas Willard, "The Gospel of the Kingdom and Spiritual Formation," *The Kingdom Life: A Practical Theology of Discipleship and Spiritual Formation*, ed. Alan Andrews (Colorado Springs, CO: NavPress, 2010), 47.

6. Dallas Willard, *The Spirit of the Disciplines: Understanding How God Changes Lives* (San Francisco, CA: HarperSanFrancisco, 1988), 65.

7. M. Robert Mulholland Jr., "Revelation," *Cornerstone Biblical Commentary*, ed. Philip W. Comfort (Carol Stream, IL: Tyndale, 2011), 526.

8. R. W. L. Moberly, "Did the Interpreters Get It Right? Genesis 2–3 Reconsidered," *Journal of Theological Studies* 59.1 (2008): 37.

9. Kinlaw, *Let's Start with Jesus*, 112.

10. F. Leron Shults and Steven J. Sandage, *Transforming Spirituality: Integrating Theology and Psychology* (Grand Rapids, MI: Baker Academic, 2006), 69.

11. James Barr, "Is God a Liar? (Genesis 2–3)—and Related Matters," *Journal of Theological Studies* 57.1 (2006): 3.

12. Moberly, "Did the Interpreters Get It Right?" 33–34.

13. John Wesley and Kenneth C. Kinghorn, *John Wesley on the Christian Practice: The Standard Sermons in Modern English* (Nashville, TN: Abingdon Press, 2003), 228.

14. Oswald Chambers, *My Utmost for His Highest: An Updated Edition in Today's English,* ed. James Reimann (Grand Rapids, MI: Discovery House, 1992), July 20.

15. Albert Cook Outler, *Theology in the Wesleyan Spirit* (Nashville, TN: Tidings, 1975), 40.

16. Shults and Sandage, *Transforming Spirituality*, 87.

Chapter 3: The Fallen Self and Its Consequences

1. Timothy C. Tennent, *The Call to Holiness: Pursuing the Heart of God for the Love of the World* (Franklin, TN: Seedbed Publishing, 2014), 27.

2. Kenneth J. Collins, *The Theology of John Wesley: Holy Love and the Shape of Grace* (Nashville, TN: Abingdon Press, 2007), 71.

3. M. Robert Mulholland Jr., *The Deeper Journey: The Spirituality of Discovering Your True Self* (Downers Grove, IL: InterVarsity, 2006), 30–42.

4. M. Robert Mulholland Jr., "Revelation," *Cornerstone Biblical Commentary*, ed. Philip W. Comfort (Carol Stream, IL: Tyndale, 2011), 564.

5. Saint Augustine, *Confessions,* trans. R. S. Pine-Coffin (London: Penguin Books, 1961), 39.

6. Thomas Merton, *The New Man* (New York: Farrar, 1962), 110.

7. Ibid., 110–11.

8. Steve DeNeff, *The Way of Holiness: Experience God's Work in You* (Indianapolis, IN: Wesleyan, 2010), 150.

9. Oswald Chambers, *My Utmost for His Highest: An Updated Edition in Today's English*, ed. James Reimann (Grand Rapids, MI: Discovery House, 1992), January 12.

10. David G. Benner, *The Gift of Being Yourself: The Sacred Call to Self-Discovery* (Downers Grove, IL: InterVarsity Press, 2004), 62.

11. Anselm Gruen, *Heaven Begins Within You: Wisdom from the Desert Fathers*, trans. Peter Heinegg (New York: Crossroad, 1999), 18.

12. Michael Glerup, "The Holy Spirit and Spiritual Formation," *The Kingdom Life: A Practical Theology of Discipleship and Spiritual Formation*, ed. Alan Andrews (Colorado Springs, CO: NavPress, 2010), 268.

13. Dallas Willard, "Spiritual Formation in Christ: A Perspective on What It Is and How It Might Be Done," *Journal of Psychology & Theology,* 28.4 (2000): 256.

14. St. Teresa of Avila and E. A. Peers, *Interior Castle* (Garden City, NJ: Doubleday, 1961), 37.

15. Michael W. Mangis, *Signature Sins: Taming our Wayward Hearts* (Downers Grove, IL: InterVarsity, 2008), 18.

16. DeNeff, *The Way of Holiness*, 204–5.

17. F. Leron Shults and Steven J. Sandage, *Transforming Spirituality: Integrating Theology and Psychology* (Grand Rapids, MI: Baker Academic, 2006), 90.

18. Mangis, *Signature Sins*, 14.

Chapter 4: Called to Holiness: The Hope of Spiritual Formation

1. Dallas Willard, *The Spirit of the Disciplines: Understanding How God Changes Lives* (San Francisco, CA: HarperSanFrancisco, 1988), 116.

2. Melvin E. Dieter, Anthony A. Hoekema, Stanley M. Horton, J. Robertson McQuilkin, and John F. Walvoord, *Five Views on Sanctification* (Grand Rapids, MI: Zondervan, 1987), 66, 125.

3. Timothy C. Tennent, *The Call to Holiness: Pursuing the Heart of God for the Love of the World* (Franklin, TN: Seedbed Publishing, 2014), 20.

4. Ibid., 27.

5. Steve DeNeff, *The Way of Holiness: Experience God's Work in You* (Indianapolis, IN: Wesleyan, 2010), 153.

6. Dieter, et al., *Five Views on Sanctification*, 195.

7. Ibid., 17.

8. Ibid., 62.

9. Ibid., 153.

10. Ibid., 135.

11. Ibid., 220–21.

12. DeNeff, *The Way of Holiness*, 121.

13. Dallas Willard, "Spiritual Formation and the Warfare Between the Flesh and the Human Spirit," *Journal of Spiritual Formation and Soul Care* Vol. 1, No. 1 (2008).

14. Dieter, et al., *Five Views on Sanctification*, 123.

15. Ibid., 185.
16. Ibid., 62.
17. Ibid., 151.
18. Ibid., 124.
19. Ibid., 220.
20. James Byron Smith, *The Good and Beautiful God* (Downers Grove, IL: IVP, 2009), 152.

Chapter 5: Transformation: The Work of the Holy Spirit

1. www.apa.org/helpcenter/willpower.pdf
2. Oswald Chambers, *My Utmost for His Highest: An Updated Edition in Today's English*, ed. James Reimann (Grand Rapids, MI: Discovery House, 1992), October 6.
3. Ibid., January 9.
4. F. Leron Shults and Steven J. Sandage, *Transforming Spirituality: Integrating Theology and Psychology* (Grand Rapids, MI: Baker Academic, 2006), 39.
5. Michael Glerup, "The Holy Spirit and Spiritual Formation," *The Kingdom Life: A Practical Theology of Discipleship and Spiritual Formation*, ed. Alan Andrews (Colorado Springs, CO: NavPress, 2010), 250.
6. Thomas à Kempis, *The Imitation of Christ in Four Books: A Translation from the Latin*, rev. ed., ed. Joseph N. Tylenda (New York: Vintage, 1998), 166.
7. Joanne Huiying Wang, "Christian Formation Within North America Protestant Christian Seminary Education," (Diss. Talbot School of Theology, Biola University, 2010), 29.
8. Shults and Sandage, *Transforming Spirituality*, 127.
9. Wang, "Christian Formation," 21.

10. Timothy C. Tennett, *The Call to Holiness: Pursuing the Heart of God for the Love of the World* (Franklin, TN: Seedbed Publishing, 2014), 44.

11. T. A. Smail, "In the Image of the Triune God," *International Journal of Systematic Theology* 5.1 (2003): 23; see Colossians 3:10.

12. Kenneth J. Collins, *The Theology of John Wesley: Holy Love and the Shape of Grace* (Nashville, TN: Abingdon Press, 2007), 202.

13. M. Robert Mulholland Jr., "Revelation," *Cornerstone Biblical Commentary*, ed. Philip W. Comfort (Carol Stream, IL: Tyndale, 2011), 492.

14. Steve DeNeff, *The Way of Holiness: Experience God's Work in You* (Indianapolis, IN: Wesleyan, 2010), 125.

15. Collins, *Theology of John Wesley*, 203.

16. John Oswalt, *Called to Be Holy* (Nappanee, IN: Evangel, 1999), 99.

17. Chambers, *My Utmost for His Highest*, February 8.

18. Steve DeNeff, *7 Saving Graces: Living Above the Deadly Sins* (Indianapolis, IN: Wesleyan, 2010), 42.

19. Peter Scazzero, *Emotionally Healthy Spirituality* (Grand Rapids, MI: Zondervan, 2006), 20. A George Barna survey indicates that only 11 percent of the population experiences a "holy discontent" with their lives and only 1 percent experience a profound love of God and people. George Barna, *Maximum Faith: Live Like Jesus* (Austin: Fedd and Company, 2011), 25.

20. Glerup, "The Holy Spirit and Spiritual Formation," 249.

21. Bill Hull, "Spiritual Formation from the Inside Out," *The Kingdom Life: A Practical Theology of Discipleship and Spiritual Formation*, ed. Alan Andrews (Colorado Springs: NavPress, 2010), 113.

22. Shults and Sandage, *Transforming Spirituality*, 83.

23. Hull, "Spiritual Formation from the Inside Out," 121.

Chapter 6: Transformation: Participation in the Work of the Holy Spirit

1. Oswald Chambers, *My Utmost for His Highest: An Updated Edition in Today's English*, ed. James Reimann (Grand Rapids, MI: Discovery House, 1992), March 18.

2. Kenneth J. Collins, *The Theology of John Wesley: Holy Love and the Shape of Grace* (Nashville, TN: Abingdon Press, 2007), 203.

3. Richard Lovelace, *Renewal as a Way of Life: A Guidebook for Spiritual Growth* (Eugene, OR: Wipf and Stock, 2002), 75.

4. Dallas Willard, *Renovation of the Heart: Putting on the Character of Christ* (Colorado Springs, CO: NavPress, 2002), 31.

5. Ibid., 109.

6. Joanne Huiying Wang, "Christian Formation Within North America Protestant Christian Seminary Education," (Diss. Talbot School of Theology, Biola University, 2010), 20.

7. Steve DeNeff, *The Way of Holiness: Experience God's Work in You* (Indianapolis, IN: Wesleyan, 2010), 65.

8. Ibid., 54.

9. Ibid.

10. Thomas Merton, *The New Man* (New York: Farrar, 1962), 237.

11. Richard E. Averbeck, "The Bible in Spiritual Formation," *The Kingdom Life: A Practical Theology of Discipleship and Spiritual Formation*, ed. Alan Andrews (Colorado Springs, CO: NavPress, 2010), 298.

12. Steve Harper, *Devotional Life in the Wesleyan Tradition* (Nashville, TN: Upper Room, 1983), 10.

13. David Teague, "The Spiritual Formation of Mission Leaders," *Evangelical Missions* Quarterly 48 (2012): 191.

14. Keith Meyer, "Whole-Life Transformation," *The Kingdom Life: A Practical Theology of Discipleship and Spiritual Formation*, ed. Alan Andrews (Colorado Springs, CO: NavPress, 2010), 146.

15. Merton, *New Man*, 237–38.

16. Ron DeBerry, "Designing an Integrative Spiritual Formation Program for Bethel College, Hampton, Virginia," (Diss. Regent University, 2007), 37.

17. Chambers, *My Utmost for His Highest*, May 8.

18. Dallas Willard, *The Spirit of the Disciplines: Understanding How God Changes Lives* (San Francisco, CA: HarperSanFrancisco, 1988), 25.

19. Bill Hull, "Spiritual Formation from the Inside Out," *The Kingdom Life: A Practical Theology of Discipleship and Spiritual Formation*, ed. Alan Andrews (Colorado Springs: NavPress, 2010), 126.

20. Dallas Willard, "Spiritual Formation in Christ: A Perspective on What It Is and How It Might Be Done," *Journal of Psychology & Theology,* 28.4 (2000): 257.

21. Willard, *Renovation of the Heart*, 109.

22. Dennis F. Kinlaw, *The Mind of Christ* (Nappanee, IN: Francis Asbury, 1998), 75.

Chapter 7: The Assurance of the Love of God

1. John R. W. Stott, *The Message of Romans: God's Good News for the World* (Leicester: InterVarsity, 1994), 145.

2. Oswald Chambers, *My Utmost for His Highest: An Updated Edition in Today's English*, ed. James Reimann (Grand Rapids, MI: Discovery House, 1992), June 5.

3. Gordon T. Smith, *The Voice of Jesus: Discernment, Prayer, and the Witness of the Spirit* (Downers Grove, IL: InterVarsity, 2003), 74.

4. Bill Thrall and Bruce McNicol, "Communities of Grace," *The Kingdom Life: A Practical Theology of Discipleship and Spiritual Formation* (Colorado Springs, CO: NavPress, 2010), 66.

5. Smith, *The Voice of Jesus*, 76.

6. M. Robert Mulholland Jr., *The Deeper Journey: The Spirituality of Discovering Your True Self* (Downers Grove, IL: InterVarsity, 2006), 79.

7. Charles de Foucauld, *Meditations of a Hermit* (London: Burns; New York: Orbis, 1981), 8.

8. David K. Clark, "Philosophical Reflections on Self-Worth and Self-Love," *Journal of Psychology & Theology* 13.1 (1985): 3.

9. Henri J. M. Nouwen, *Life of the Beloved: Spiritual Living in a Secular World* (New York: Crossroad, 1992), 31.

10. Clark, "Philosophical Reflections on Self-Worth and Self-Love," 5.

11. John Lippitt, "True Self-Love and True Self-Sacrifice," *International Journal for Philosophy of Religion* 3.125 (2009): 132.

12. Nouwen, *Life of the Beloved*, 56.

13. Henri J. M. Nouwen, *The Return of the Prodigal Son: A Story of Homecoming* (New York: Doubleday, 1992), 16ff.

14. Mulholland, *Deeper Journey*, 119.